public libraries
and resilient cities

public libraries and resilient cities

edited by Michael Dudley

American Library Association
Chicago • 2013

Michael Dudley is the indigenous and urban services librarian at the University of Winnipeg and the editorial board chair for *Plan Canada* magazine, the official publication of the Canadian Institute of Planners.

Printed in the United States of America
17 16 15 14 13   5 4 3 2 1

Extensive effort has gone into ensuring the reliability of the information in this book; however, the publisher makes no warranty, express or implied, with respect to the material contained herein.

ISBNs: 978-0-8389-1136-5 (paper); 978-0-8389-9612-6 (PDF); 978-0-8389-9613-3 (ePub); 978-0-8389-9614-0 (Kindle). For more information on digital formats, visit the ALA Store at alastore.ala.org and select eEditions.

Library of Congress Cataloging-in-Publication Data

Public libraries and resilient cities / edited by Michael Dudley.
   pages   cm
     Includes bibliographical references and index.
     ISBN 978-0-8389-1136-5 (alk. paper)
     1. Libraries and metropolitan areas. 2. Libraries and metropolitan areas—
United States. I. Dudley, Michael (Michael Q.), editor of compilation.
   Z716.2.P82 2013
   021'.2—dc23   2012019788

Cover design by Karen Sheets de Gracia.
Cover illustration © Cienpies Design/Shutterstock, Inc.
Book design by Kimberly Thornton in Helvetica Neue and Minion Pro.

⊚ This paper meets the requirements of ANSI/NISO Z39.48-1992 (Permanence of Paper).

For Karen and Tiryn
Thank you for reminding me that I am not a gadget.

contents

preface

n the midst of an economic and technological "perfect storm," the public library is increasingly being seen as a keystone institution in addressing a number of significant and pressing urban and environmental sustainability issues. Libraries are evolving sustainable urban design practices, ecologically sensitive procurement processes, contributing to local economic development, and adapting to rapidly changing conditions, all while maintaining a strong commitment to social equity. From the economic renewal potential of library development projects, to the provision of public space in a privatizing world, to targeting services for the homeless and crisis management during natural (and other) disasters, public libraries have shown themselves capable of contributing to community resiliency—that is, the ability of a community to respond effectively to stressors and challenging circumstances.

This book, *Public Libraries and Resilient Cities,* will explore the roles that public libraries can play in the promotion of ecologically, economically, and socially resilient communities in challenging times. It situates the public library in terms of urban planning concepts as well as current thinking on sustainability issues, and shares success stories in resiliency from library and planning practitioners. For the librarian, this book will hopefully reinforce and strengthen what is already known about the potentialities of the public library, while providing new contexts for its contribution. For the urban and regional planner, this book will demonstrate that the public library is a valuable partner in promoting planning goals.

The collection of essays in this book is intended to demonstrate that public libraries can contribute to a city's diversity, adaptability, and learning capacity. While there is a long tradition in the library literature arguing for the public library's role in addressing urban social problems, I believe the gravity of our contemporary social, environmental, and economic crises constitutes a renewed and urgent imperative for such an engagement—made more so by the constraints and challenges of economic recession and fiscal retrenchment on the part of governments.

By highlighting case studies of innovation in public library design, management, collaboration, and public services, I hope that *Public Libraries and Resilient Cities* will provide librarians, library administrators, and urban planners with the knowledge, tools, and vocabulary to bridge professional and disciplinary barriers, and to recognize and promote the importance of the public library to successful, equitable, and sustainable cities. Public libraries, it will be argued, are contributing meaningfully to "placemaking," or the creation and nurturing of vital and unique communities that can provide intergenerational equity for their residents. This book will consider the public library—as an institution, a place, a function, and an idea—as one important means by which cities may develop resilience. It considers both precedent and potentialities for public libraries to serve the needs of their communities in terms of increasing their flexibility, diversity, interconnections, and adaptability through contributing to their learning capacity, even as those communities and their needs undergo dramatic change.

In the pages that follow, the contributing authors and myself will demonstrate these synergies. In chapter one I will review some of the major trends facing contemporary urban societies and their public libraries before introducing key concepts in resilience and how they can relate to the public library's mission. With these foundations in place, we then turn to the work of the book's contributors, who for the most part describe their own experiences working in public libraries under challenging circumstances, whether these are straitened economic conditions or outright disaster. In these pages you will learn of efforts to address poverty and social exclusion; to recover from disaster; and to build environmentally sustainable communities.

A number of these themes have, of course, already been addressed in the library literature, and indeed some of them have been currents in the literature for decades; yet in recent years they have come to the forefront. Sanford Berman (2007) and Karen M. Venturella (1998) have urged a greater role for libraries in services to the urban poor, and Kathleen de la Peña McCook showed how libraries can contribute to community building (2000), while Ronald McCabe (2001) has argued for renewing the social mission of the public library in the face of growing social problems.[1] Roger Kemp and Marcia Trotta (2008) examined the role libraries play in urban vitality; Shannon Mattern studied the prominence of new downtown libraries in placemaking (2007); and Kathryn Miller highlighted the ability of public libraries to "green" their operations (2010) to become more sustainable.[2]

The context for the present exploration, however, is that of crisis, both within the library world and the larger society. For that reason its scope is necessarily constrained. Just as cities and their flows of information and commodities are best viewed in terms of their complexity, so too is the relationship between the city and the public library a complex one: it is multifaceted, mutual, dynamic, and one structured by law, convention, and culture. The influences on the public library are many and have been approached from a wide variety of perspectives by countless authors over decades, as we have seen. A thorough and holistic examination of the public library's relationship with urban conditions would of necessity include discussions of the education system, literacy, democracy, culture, technology, social changes, community economic development, moral values, community capacity, public administration, poverty, and homelessness, to say nothing of architecture and urban planning. Most of these are beyond the scope offered here. My treatment of the broad themes related to the library-city interface in the introduction is deliberately focused on the library and the city in particular, rather than these issues in general.

The intention is not so much to identify innovative public library contributions to community development, ecological sustainability, or social equity, for these areas have been well established by others. Rather, the focus is to explore how such innovations can contribute to a city's ability to *respond to stressors*—whatever they may be. I am interested here in potentialities. What follows is both suggestive and normative, rather than empirical. In other words, I'm not out to "prove" through a collection of essays that a public library *has,* in a particular instance, made a city more resilient than it otherwise might have been without one. Instead—and in the context of anticipated transformations—I am arguing for the *necessity* of the public library as a keystone municipal institution, and that this necessity derives from both the library's traditional functions as well as emerging ones.

While contributions in this collection derive from the United States, Canada, Europe, and Africa, there is a geographic and political emphasis on the contexts in the United States. Not only does the balance of the selections describe the American experience, but the crises facing cities and public libraries emerging from both the global recession and the politicization of urban development and publicly funded institutions are in so advanced a state in America that the book's themes are particularly pertinent there. Canada, by virtue of its more regulated banking and real estate industries, has been to a large extent shielded from the full brunt of the present recession; yet its peculiarly impoverished constitutional arrangements where cities are concerned leave its municipalities even more hamstrung than their American counterparts. While Canadian public libraries have for the most part not faced the same debilitating budget cuts as those in the United States, the contributions and partnerships of which public libraries are capable are just as relevant for Canadian libraries and cities.

This project warrants a little background. It's the product of bridging two professions: I am both a librarian and a city planner. For five years I worked for the Edmonton Public Library in Alberta in a number of capacities, and completed a master's degree in library and information studies at the University of Alberta before moving to Calgary to work for the public library there for four more years. Having fielded during those years thousands of reference questions, visited schools, delivered book readings, performed puppet shows, and read stories to preschoolers, I found rewards in every setting and was unsure in what capacity I would ultimately end up working.

In the course of commuting by bicycle to my job at the Calgary Public Library (CPL) I became politicized regarding transportation issues and soon became engrossed in reading urban studies literature. After coordinating the CPL's participation in that city's commuter challenge for a couple of years, I came to the realization that many of the issues that engaged my attention were urban ones. I can still recall the moment in 1997 when I knew that I had to pursue the city professionally. I was riding the train, reading the closing pages of Jane Jacobs's classic book *The Death and Life of Great American Cities*, when I came across her famous final line: "lively, diverse, intense cities contain the seeds of their own regeneration, with energy enough to carry over for problems and needs outside themselves."[3]

Within a year my wife and I had sold our house and moved to Winnipeg, where I enrolled in the city planning graduate program at the University of Manitoba. As much as I had loved being a public librarian, I felt compelled to understand the problems of the city and hoped to someday be able to address them. I never expected to work in a library again, but as fortune would have it, shortly after graduating I received a phone call from the then-director of the Institute of Urban Studies at the University of Winnipeg. They had an urban planning library but nobody to run it; would I be interested?

Since 2001 this hybridized career has served me very well; but I have never lost sight of the recognition that the worlds of the library and the city share more than most realize: not only are the fortunes of libraries and their communities intertwined, but because of these synergies, some of the professional interests of the planner and librarian are similarly parallel. An understanding of and engagement with community are therefore paramount to the mission of both professions, as is the goal of creating vital and livable communities.

In the following pages we will learn about the ways in which the public library, in partnership with other institutions and with citizens, contributes to the ability of urban areas to respond to challenges—in other words, to be resilient. Yet this relationship can only flourish where public libraries themselves are allowed to do so as well—and in our present era of shrinking budgets and ideologically motivated attacks on public services this is very much in doubt.

Public libraries must weather this crisis and aid their cities in the process. Inasmuch as libraries are institutions dependent on public funding, they are much more than mere outlets of service delivery; they are a cultural force both ancient and modern, repositories of wisdom and whimsy and, when used to their full potential, generators of innovation, creativity, and new visions for the future.

My hope, then, is that in the pages below we can see how—to crib from Jane Jacobs—*"lively, diverse, intense public libraries contain the seeds of their own regeneration, with energy enough to carry over for problems and needs outside themselves."*

—Michael Dudley

NOTES

1. Sanford Berman, "Classicism in the Stacks: Libraries and Poverty," *Journal of Information Ethics* (Spring 2007): 103–10; Karen M. Venturella, *Poor People and Library Services* (Jefferson, NC: McFarland, 1998); Kathleen de la Peña McCook,

A Place at the Table: Participating in Community Building (Chicago: American Library Association, 2000); Ronald McCabe, *Civic Librarianship: Renewing the Social Mission of the Public Library* (Lanham, MD: Scarecrow, 2001).

2. Roger L. Kemp and Marcia Trotta, *Museums, Libraries and Urban Vitality* (Jefferson, NC: McFarland, 2008); Shannon Christine Mattern, *The New Downtown Library: Designing with Communities* (Minneapolis: University of Minnesota Press, 2007); Kathryn Miller, *Public Libraries Going Green* (Chicago: American Library Association, 2010).

3. Jane Jacobs, *The Death and Life of Great American Cities* (New York: Random House, 1961), 448.

acknowledgments

would like first of all to thank my editor at ALA Editions, Christopher Rhodes, for inviting me to propose a project that, unbeknownst to him, had been on my mind for more than a decade. Chris was extremely supportive and appreciative of the complexity of the project. And he wouldn't have come across my name had not Carol Smallwood accepted my contributions to her 2010 book, *Writing and Publishing: The Librarian's Handbook.* (Thanks Carol!)

A big debt of gratitude goes to the Urban Libraries Council (ULC), which not only contributed a chapter (in the form of an adaptation of their report *Partners for the Future*) but, through the terrific Veronda Pitchford and Mary Colleen Bragiel, provided additional information and referral to potential authors (hey, isn't that what librarians do?).

That I was able to take advantage of the ULC's expertise in this area is owed to the support of the University of Winnipeg. The dean of libraries, Jane Duffy, and Dr. Jino Distasio, the director of the Institute of Urban Studies (IUS), cost-shared IUS's membership in ULC, which afforded the project several key contacts. Furthermore, Dr. Distasio graciously allowed me to work on this project on institute time, and using the institute's resources, which was a huge support.

I would also like to thank all of my contributors for offering such excellent and diverse chapters for the book. I'm extremely honored to have obtained the involvement of so many recognized leaders in the field, and thanks to them the project became far richer than I'd originally hoped.

Thanks go to both my wife Karen and my parents Harry and Nancy for taking the first crack at reviewing my own contributions. Their sharp eyes and critiques made the preface and introduction much stronger than they would have been otherwise.

Finally—and especially—I wish to thank Karen and my daughter Tiryn for their love, support, patience, and humor through the long months during which I woke up far too early to write and edit and became a tad grumpy from lack of sleep. They as much as anyone helped me in making the book a reality.

chapter one

Michael Dudley

The library and the city

Libraries stand as a prime example of social capital, which more and more observers see as the secret sauce that makes the difference between a community that thrives and one that struggles.

—Jay Walljasper

From crisis to resilience

Braddock, Pennsylvania, was the site of the first of the over 1,600 public libraries that Andrew Carnegie would construct in the United States. Built to serve the needs of the workers at the magnate's Edgar Thomson Steel Works, the Carnegie Free Library of Braddock is a majestic brownstone structure that is still a focal point for the town. Originally constructed in 1888—with a subsequent addition only five years later—the library housed bathing and recreational facilities for Carnegie's steelworkers, including a swimming pool, a gymnasium, and a music hall, as well as the requisite books. Fueled by the steel industry, Braddock was a rapidly growing industrial center, and its population would reach 20,000 people in the 1920s before a gradual decline in the postwar years turned precipitous in the 1970s following the collapse of the American steel industry.

The Braddock Carnegie Library would languish along with its community: its roof gave way in the 1970s and its interior fell into disrepair from exposure to the elements. Even though it had been added to the National Register of Historic Places in 1973, it still faced demolition, and it was not until later that decade that the local Field Historical Society led a grassroots campaign to save the structure and bought it from the town for one dollar.

However, Braddock's woes continued to worsen: by the turn of the twenty-first century, and having lost nearly 90 percent of its population and been ravaged by an epidemic of crack cocaine, Braddock became the very epitome of Rust Belt decline. Yet the Braddock Carnegie Library remained open—for all practical purposes the only functioning institution left in town. As the *New York Times* describes it, the library, along with "a medical clinic, auto garages, a florist, an optometrist, three markets, a preschool, a parochial school [and] a dollar store . . . continue[s] to do business alongside empty buildings wrapped in barbed wire."[1]

The Braddock Carnegie Library may have a long history and its share of brushes with erasure, but it has emerged confidently into the twenty-first century: its Facebook page and Flickr account give ample evidence of its imaginative and innovative programming, including art classes, printmaking, music lessons, line dancing, ceramics studio, cooking classes, and community feasts. The town's fortunes have also been boosted by the creativity of its energetic mayor, John Fetterman, whose "do-it-yourself" revitalization efforts made him a media favorite and caught the attention of the Levi Strauss Company. In fact, Levi's in 2010 made the town and its mayor the subject of a multimillion-dollar "Ready to Work" series of short films, part of which focused on the library and its programming, and how the library had become, in their words, "a symbol of the town's resilience."[2]

As the Braddock experience illustrates, the development and resilience of cities and towns have always been bound up with that of their libraries; after all, urbanism itself originated in part from the creation and storage of written records and the correspondingly complex societies those records made possible.[3] By *resilience* we mean the ability of cities, towns, or neighborhoods to respond effectively to changing circumstances and challenges by virtue of their flexibility, diversity, and built-in redundancies. While we often hear of resilience in the face of disaster or crisis, its application need not be so extreme: it pertains instead to a system's inherent organic quality, allowing it, like a successful species or an enduring habitat in the natural world, to continue to maintain its primary functions even as its circumstances change.

An understanding of resilience speaks to the nature of a city's interconnections, as well as its adaptability and learning capacity. In the pages to follow, we will consider how public libraries can contribute to enriching these interconnections, to building a community's adaptive capabilities, and to enhancing learning capacity. In their long-established roles of supporting both informed decision making and genuine democratic processes, as well as the ability of citizens to access the range of information, services, and opportunities that may only be had in the public realm, public libraries surely play a leading role in bolstering urban resiliency.

Discussions about different concepts related to resiliency have gained a great deal of currency in recent years as the challenges confronting urban societies have grown more urgent. Rapid urbanization, escalating poverty, depleting energy resources, climate change, and ever-worsening gridlock have led many to question how cities can be made more livable in the twenty-first century; but their proposals must contend with divergent and competing visions for the metropolis.

One of these visions is associated with a form of urbanism found the world over: a relatively dense population, with buildings four to six stories tall; a mix of shops, businesses, and services within walking distance; a variety of means to travel; streets filled with a diverse combination of people of all ages; and abundant public spaces. In this city, differences are accommodated more readily because there are so many of them; behaviors are more liberated because of sheer anonymity; and opportunities and choices are readily at hand. Houses, apartments, and shops share the same block, and the yards, if they exist, are small and feature front-facing porches that allow neighbors to engage one another in conversation. Since everything can be reached on foot, independence costs relatively little. The businesses and services are of modest scale and owned by local residents. And the public realm is everything: with private space at a premium, social activities and recreation are largely enjoyed in the company of others. This is the kind of cityspace that Canadian author Chris Turner calls the classic "urban operating system," one that has proved its durability over hundreds and thousands of years, across cultures and across continents.[4]

The other vision is perhaps more familiar to most North American readers: a city divided into zones, with single-family housing congregated by income level and at great distances from apartments; corporate retail "power centers" clustered at major freeway intersections, yet far enough apart and in such hostile surroundings that walking from one to the other would be inconvenient at best and dangerous at worst; employment centers even further away from home, requiring long and solitary commutes by car; and the whole set of functional pods stitched together with freeways. Because housing is grouped by price point, social division and de facto segregation are inevitable. A great number of life opportunities and choices may be available, but at a price paid in time and distance. The private realm dominates, with rear-facing decks and private pools outside and home theaters inside. In this city, independence comes dear; car ownership is required. Public transit, if it is available at all, is infrequent and tediously slow. This city space is dubbed by author James Howard Kunstler as "the Geography of Nowhere," and one that has almost no prospects for viability in a world running out of cheap fossil fuels.[5]

The debate over the direction of the city is very much an open one, and under the best of conditions has always been made problematic by economic competition between cities and their suburbs, often taking the form of a "race to the bottom" in terms of tax rates and concessions to developers. However, this debate has morphed into one not so much about urban form as it is about the nature of American society itself, and the extent to which our freedoms as individuals to live and work where we choose may be infringed upon in an era of dwindling resources. For many, the postwar suburb, with its curvilinear streets devoted exclusively to single-family homes, represents the American Dream and all that comes with it. Any notion that we live in a world of limits, and that this living arrangement may soon be rendered dysfunctional and crippled by such threats as "peak oil" and climate change, is regarded by many opponents of sustainability planning as liberal, elitist claptrap, or in the words of libertarian author Wendell Cox, a "War on the Dream."[6]

On the other side, advocates for a return to traditional urbanism—for what is popularly known as New Urbanism—see an urgent need to increase the density of our cities, to make better provisions for walking, cycling, and public transit, and for regulations to rein in urban growth, redirecting it inward so as to preserve open space and—critically—farmland.

These worldviews are increasingly at odds and unable to communicate. Worse, the nature and future of the metropolis have, in fact, become inextricably bound up with America's "culture wars" and hence, with its notions of itself as a democracy. The role and extent of governments and markets, the rights and responsibilities of the individual, and the relationship between humans and nature—all these are fundamental to a functioning democracy yet are becoming increasingly contested as both financial and natural resources dwindle; as governments, mass media, and other institutions have lost their credibility; and as ideological extremism undermines certain formerly shared values and assumptions about what constitutes a good society.

There is, however, one North American institution that has always served to mediate such forces in the culture, and that is the public library. Replete with a tradition of both progressive and conserving impulses yet holding a steadfast commitment to an informed electorate and strong democracies, the public library stands as a public institution—indeed one of the few remaining public institutions—that may be credibly seen as a force for reason, insight, wisdom, and inspiration. Not incidentally, it is equally at home in central cities, suburbs, and towns of all sizes. It also finds itself at a historical moment when it is both wildly popular and needed more than ever, but is nevertheless threatened by forces ideologically predisposed to erode it financially, and technologies and economic logic seemingly bent on usurping its purpose.

Like the cities in which they are situated, public libraries are facing challenges—and in some cases, the same challenges. In a time of collapsing civic and state budgets in the United States and a volatile political climate, the long-term survival of the public library in its present form cannot be guaranteed. Like Marylaine Block, author of *The Thriving Library*, I fear for the future of the public library owing to the "perfect storm" it is facing.[7] Carl Grant summarizes the situation this way:

> Libraries are being closed; hours reduced, funding slashed, staff reduced, collections purged, and programs are being eliminated. Beyond the financial crisis with which libraries are already dealing, there are the much larger country-wide issues of a failing commercial real estate market, growing unemployment, and numerous states that are facing bankruptcy. If any of these situations worsens, it will require more federal bailouts and almost certainly it will mean that we will all be facing inflation and further devaluation of our currency. And, each one of those crises will have a continuing major negative impact on libraries as we know them today.[8]

Crushing debt on the part of American city and state governments is resulting in public library funding being squeezed like never before. As this book was being prepared, New Jersey's Camden Library shuttered one branch and turned its library over to the county; the Detroit Public Library laid off more than eighty staff after a failed fund-raising effort that yielded a mere $100.00; California's Governor Jerry Brown handed down a budget that sliced more than $30 million from public library funding; and the state of Texas passed a budget in May 2011 that all but killed state support for public libraries, and left a mere 1 percent of former funding in place. In Santa Clarita, California, three libraries were privatized and handed over to Library Systems and Services, a company that already operates formerly public libraries in Oregon, Florida, Tennessee, Texas, and Kansas. During the battle over the federal budget in the spring of 2011, New Jersey Republican Representative Scott Garrett introduced a motion—which was defeated—that would have entirely eliminated funding for the Institute of Museum and Library Services (IMLS) and the Library Services and Technology Act (LSTA), upon which America's public libraries depend for federal funding.

These issues are hardly confined to the United States. In Canada, Toronto's public library, threatened with significant cuts under the new administration of conservative mayor Rob Ford, was forced to close its Urban Affairs Branch and reduce hours throughout the system, retrenchments which would only mark the beginning of an ongoing battle over its future. And in the United Kingdom, the austere "Comprehensive Spending Review" of the Cameron-Clegg coalition government will likely lead to the closure of at least 400 public libraries, with the possibility of 600 more in the next three years.[9] And with Greece, Spain, Portugal, and Italy all facing default, publicly funded services of all kinds are facing an extremely uncertain future.

In response to these dire trends, Art Brodsky (of the information society lobbying group Public Knowledge) warned during 2010's National Library Week that America's "Public Library lifeline was fraying" because libraries are not seen as an "essential" service but as a discretionary one.[10] Glen Holt concurs, noting that the tradition of public libraries being "free" has led to the popular misconception that they don't require taxpayer support—and besides, since the Internet is "free" then libraries ought to be, as well. Holt adds:

> Technology and the economy have reshaped the "marketplace" for libraries. We really do have competition—pottery stores that give children's story times and an Internet that revises information faster than our staff can provide it [with] headings. And information and books and magazines are distributed faster than ever. We don't read daily newspapers because it is like reading boring history text books. We use syndicated electronic feeds from our favorite communities and blog interpreters to hear the voices we like to hear to offset the pontifical "experts" who in their print pieces act like we have no other sources of news. Where does the library fit into these massive shifts?[11]

An indicator of this disrespect may be seen in an infamous news story broadcast on a Fox News affiliate in the summer of 2010 which suggested that the tax money that was going to public libraries would be better spent on schools, police, or pensions.[12]

The crisis of the public library does not end with mere budget cuts, as significant as they are. As a consequence of the economic downturn brought on by the foreclosure crisis and the collapse of Wall Street in 2008, as well as the resurgent right-wing rhetoric that exploits it, the very *notion* of the "public" has come under attack, be it in the form of taxes, services, publicly funded health care, Social Security, or salaries for public employees. The "Tea Party" insurgency that in 2010 boosted Republican fortunes and filled the party's ranks in Congress has lent even more political will to the efforts to roll back most of the achievements of the New Deal. The highest-profile test case for this agenda has been the state of Wisconsin, where Governor Scott Walker legislated an end to most collective bargaining rights for public workers and championed the privatization of education.[13]

This neoliberal logic is forcing pronounced and debilitating divisions between the private and the public realms and, as a consequence, the erosion of the latter. In an increasingly privatized urban society where the private sector is lionized and any notion of the "commons" is essentially equated in some quarters with socialism, the public library appears extremely vulnerable. As educator Henry Giroux writes:

> Shared sacrifice and shared responsibilities now give way to shared fears and a disdain for investing in the common good. Conservatives and liberals alike seem to view public values, public spheres and the notion of the common good as either a hindrance to the profit-seeking goals of a market-driven society or a drain on the market-driven social order, treated as a sign of weakness, if not pathology, or even worse, dangerous. . . . As social problems are privatized and public spaces commodified, there has been an increased emphasis on individual solutions to socially produced problems, while at the same time market relations and the commanding institutions of capital are divorced from matters of politics, ethics and responsibility.[14]

These conditions are equally at work in America's cities. What began as a foreclosure crisis in 2007–08 has erupted into a full-blown recession that has left millions out of work, thousands of homes abandoned—many of them still unbuilt in what are now "ghost" subdivisions—and increasing numbers of families entering the ranks of the homeless. In 2010 the Conference of Mayors reported an average 9 percent increase in family homelessness in American cities, and services are so overwhelmed that 64 percent of cities reported their shelters are regularly turning families away.[15] With states unable to run deficits and struggling to fund their operations in a climate hostile to public taxation or public investments of any kind, they are instituting massive cutbacks to their cities, and many municipalities are reaching the point where they will be unable to raise capital by issuing bonds, and indeed many are on the brink of defaulting on existing bonds. One of the most dire results is that the American Society of Civil Engineers estimates that the United States has an infrastructure deficit of over $2 trillion, owed not only to aging roads, bridges, and sewer lines, but to decades' worth of neglect from all levels of government. At the same time, global resources and geopolitical circumstances are driving up the cost of petroleum-based energy and building materials, just as the threat of global climate change has made new investments in more sustainable infrastructure an urgent priority.[16]

On a global scale, environmental conditions are worsening rapidly. In 2010–11 we witnessed a series of devastating climate-related disasters as much of the Northern Hemisphere baked under extreme heat while the South suffered heavy rains. An unprecedented heat wave in Russia incinerated forests and left as many as 15,000 dead, leading to a halt in Russian grain exports. Flooding in Pakistan covered a fifth of the country, injured or displaced 21 million people, and killed nearly 2,000. Over 3,000 people perished in floods and mudslides in China, and millions of Nigerians were displaced by flooding in September. An enormous section of the Petermann Glacier in Greenland broke away in August 2010, and between December and January three-quarters of the state of Queensland in Australia was hit by massive flooding that killed at least thirty-five people and caused an estimated $30-billion hit to Australia's economy—which was already affected by the lethal 2009 brushfires in the state of Victoria that killed 173 people, following almost ten years of drought. In June 2011, the Internal Displacement Monitoring Centre determined that approximately 42 million people worldwide had fled their homes due to environmental natural disasters in 2010, an increase of 17 million over 2009.[17]

Accompanying these natural disasters—many of them exacerbated by anthropogenic climate change—have been some equally devastating technological calamities. The Deepwater Horizon blowout dominated headlines for much of the middle of 2010 as millions of barrels of oil and highly toxic dispersants fouled the Gulf of Mexico, even as a public information crisis developed around the unknown risks to public health. A similarly prolonged and globally significant disaster befell the Fukushima-Daiichi nuclear reactor in Japan following the devastating Tohoku earthquake and tsunami of March 11, 2011, which killed almost 16,000 people. As of this writing, with reliable public information on the disaster disturbingly scant, the reactors are still spewing radioactivity and engineers speculate that the decommissioning process will take decades.

Taken together, these events point to a future of growing crises—of ever more extreme weather events for which our societies are ill-prepared, and energy regimes demanding ever more risky and hazardous practices, portending further and perhaps even more widespread spills or meltdowns. What's more, they illustrate how, even in our "information age," corporations and governments alike can stifle and obfuscate badly needed information that is in the public interest.

In her 2002 book, *Planning in the Face of Crisis,* Israeli planner Rachelle Alterman reviews the literature on crisis and disaster planning and identifies key attributes of crisis situations requiring special attention in planning, several of which I elaborate on below.[18]

High degree of uncertainty and dependence on exogenous variables. Geological, environmental, and geopolitical conditions around the world have an impact on local conditions and cannot be excluded from planning processes. Where community planners in the past might have focused solely on local demographic or economic data, now conditions are influenced by a host of global factors that are all interconnected and therefore subject to feedback loops. The price for gasoline, for example, has risen and fallen dramatically and unpredictably in recent years, with almost immediate impacts on agriculture and shipping and therefore the affordability and availability of food.

High degree of change. Just as changes to local communities are increasingly global, so too are these changes more dramatic and disruptive—the scale and extent of climate-related catastrophes being only the most obvious. However, the anticipated peaking of the global oil supply will bring with it significant changes to almost every aspect of our globalized society, from transportation to food production to the availability of everyday goods.

Low degree of knowledge and understanding; existing solutions inadequate. Having based planning decisions for so many decades on the basis of stable economies, predictable weather, and cheap and dependable energy, existing processes and institutions are not prepared for the challenges that economic, social, and environmental crises may bring. Our institutions, businesses, and democracies—if they are to thrive in the twenty-first century—will be forced to innovate and adapt to these conditions or else they will fail.

Challenge on the "symbolic" level (goals, norms, and values); low degree of goal consensus. Part of the reason that our institutions, economies, and practices are not commensurate with the challenges currently facing our globalized society is that the status quo is powerfully supported by sociopolitical ideologies for which concepts such as climate change and peak oil represent threats not so much to the future of humanity as they do to that status quo. The suburban development model which has so dominated our cities for decades is seen as being particularly vulnerable as energy becomes more expensive; yet it is so enmeshed with our notions of the "American Dream" that its partisans are hostile to any alternative. Many Republicans, for example, refuse to accept the legitimacy of climate science, because to do so would require calling into question almost everything they believe is essential to a strong American economy. As Naomi Klein observes, accepting the reality of climate change

> would mean upending the whole free trade agenda, because it would mean that we would have to localize our economies, because we have the most energy-inefficient trade system that you could imagine. . . . That would have to be reversed. You would have to deal with inequality. You would have to redistribute wealth, because this is a crisis that was created in the North, and the effects are being felt in the South. So, on the most basic, basic, "you broke it, you bought it," polluter pays, you would have to redistribute wealth, which is also against their ideology. You would have to regulate corporations. You simply would have to. I mean, any serious climate action has to intervene in the economy. You would have to subsidize renewable energy, which also breaks their worldview. You would have to have a really strong United Nations, because individual countries can't do this alone. You absolutely have to have a strong international architecture. So when you go through this, you see, it challenges everything that they believe in.[19]

What we see, then, is a world in which crises are global and multiplying in complexity and intensity, but derive from contested causes that often threaten us on a symbolic level, thereby forestalling any resolution. Furthermore, efforts to challenge the dominant political economy through popular movements such as Occupy Wall Street become, themselves, threats to this symbolic level of individual and collective identities.

There is, however, one starting point upon which many can agree: if the economic, social, and ecological challenges of the twenty-first century are going to be addressed at all, they will need to be addressed in, with, and through the world's cities. In his 2009 book, *Welcome to the Urban Revolution*, Jeb Brugmann puts it this way:

> If we can just learn how to design, govern, and manage the growth of our cities, we can also design solutions to many of the global problems that confront us. But if we fail to advance sound practices of urbanism . . . we will be designing the global crises of tomorrow.[20]

To meet the challenges posed by these crises, what many urban planners are arguing for now is a transition to a sustainable society—one with the resilience necessary to adapt to the changes ahead. While *resiliency* may contribute to a city's *sustainability*, it is important that we distinguish between them. As a term, *sustainability* has of course become ubiquitous since the United Nations' World Commission on Environment and Development defined it in 1987 as "development that meets the needs of the present without compromising the ability of future generations to meet their own needs."[21] It therefore is generally applied to *forms of development*, characterizing them as having the capacity to meet present and future needs in a balanced and equitable fashion. Sustainability in turn is comprised not just of environmental sensitivity, but economic and social qualities as well—with the stipulation that development should not only boost a community's economy, but preserve or enhance the ecological bases of that community while at the same time distributing resources more equitably.

Cities, on the other hand, are more than a mere type of development. They are complex, constantly evolving collaborations between thousands or millions of people, all of whom are interacting, sharing, and competing over flows of commodities, energy, and information within ecological and material constraints, and under a wide range of governance styles. It is therefore more accurate to refer to cities as *systems*, rather than as static developments, which necessitates a more holistic and dynamic way of describing them. Systems-thinking also requires us to be more process-oriented, rather than geared toward an ideal end-state, as is the case with sustainability. As Andrew McMurray writes,

> Resilience implies action: to be resilient. Resilience implies an inner toughness: the strength, as its etymology tells us, to jump back to a previous state. Sustainability, by contrast, suggests a defensive posture, a desire to stay the same, to resist change without the attractive ability to push back against change and win out. Resilience also connotes

a measure of risk, while sustainability suggests that systems are set: they simply need to be cared for and so carried forward. Resilience acknowledges that risk is a constant, and that systems are always in a struggle against dissipation.[22]

Generally, resilience is understood as the degree to which a complex system is flexible enough to respond and adapt to an externally imposed force or change and thus persist over time while retaining its structure and functions. Conversely, a vulnerable system would be one in which conditions are inflexible, key resources comprise a monoculture, there is little learning capacity, and choices for addressing crises are constrained.

Resilience can be manifested in both ecologies and in human societies; each are considered highly complex systems in which the interrelationships and synergies between elements are fundamentally important to their potential resiliency. Human societies are indivisible from their bases in the natural environment: social-ecological systems such as cities cannot therefore be considered resilient unless these adaptive capacities are present not only in the natural environment but also within the full range of social, cultural, economic, and political relationships.

Highly interconnected systems such as cities, economies, or global ecosystems are seen to be vulnerable because failure in one part of a system can reinforce collapse in another. This can then result in a cascading series of failures. To address these possibilities, resilience principles emphasize self-organization, flexibility, and adaptation through redundancy, distribution of resources, and the development of learning capacity, as well as a loosening of interconnections, making a system (be it a forest or a city) better capable of bearing and absorbing shocks.

In the early years of the twenty-first century several significant and devastating events contributed to a heightened interest in the use of biological models for understanding and repairing social-ecological systems. The terrorist attacks of September 11, 2001, on New York and Washington D.C. shocked the world and revealed not only the inherent risk in centralizing operations and resources, but that cities are vulnerable to volatile global geopolitics. Less than two years later the blackout of August 2003 knocked out power to millions of people from Toronto to New York to Detroit, demonstrating the dangerous overextension of North America's outdated and centralized energy technologies. Then the devastation wrought by Hurricane Katrina on New Orleans and the Gulf Coast in 2005 was exacerbated in equal parts by the prior destruction of coastal wetlands for development, the poor state of infrastructure intended to protect New Orleans, and the many social inequities that left thousands of African American residents with no means of escape.

In light of these and other cases of disaster and recovery, the recent literature on hazard mitigation advocates strategies to promote urban resilience, such as ensuring reserves of key resources; equitably distributed and redundant infrastructure; and healthy social networks of trust to ensure people can share information and come to one another's aid.[23] Urban resilience is also viewed in terms of our uncertain future and how human societies might cope with peak oil and climate change. Accordingly, the resilient city of the twenty-first century will need to include renewable energy; carbon neutrality; dispersed utilities such as small-scale solar and wind rather than massive, centralized power plants; local agricultural and fiber production; closed-loop industries in which one manufacturing process uses the waste or by-products of another; local economies focusing on independent and locally owned businesses rather than being dominated by distant mega-corporations; and a transportation hierarchy built around compact urban environments supportive of walking, cycling, public transportation, and electric vehicles.[24]

The concept of resilience saw its origins during the early 1970s in the ecological sciences. Canadian ecologist Crawford "Buzz" Holling used mathematical models of natural systems to determine what makes them adaptive and resilient. Holling observed that forests have an adaptive cycle of growth, conservation, collapse, regeneration, and regrowth. In the growth stage the ecosystem gathers biomass and becomes increasingly complex and interconnected. Eventually, self-regulation mechanisms kick in, developing efficiencies as specialized organisms fill a range of niches, and the system seeks to conserve these efficiencies. Eventually, however, the forest becomes so oriented to a particular and specific set of environmental circumstances that it can't absorb shocks, be they invasive species or changes to climatic conditions. The introduction of such elements—particularly if the result of violent or abrupt change—can therefore cause collapse of the ecosystem.[25]

Yet in the wake of this collapse comes the opportunity for new organisms to gain hold, which at first are not interconnected to others and so can develop independently. With the arrival of these new opportunistic organisms the system experiences regeneration and reorganization, as well as the beginning of a new growth stage. The ability of such a system to so regenerate also depends on the health of larger-scale complex systems in which they reside; if the climate is stable, the forest will regenerate.

Holling was careful to distinguish between system equilibrium and resiliency. That an ecosystem is stable does not mean it can persist indefinitely; in fact, he argued that long-term homogenous conditions work against resilience by reducing diversity and flexibility, thereby discouraging novelty. By contrast, a resilient system may fluctuate greatly in terms of its condition and populations, but it nonetheless, over time, will demonstrate a greater ability to persist. Resilience is therefore not the result of any one element in the system but the nature of the relationship between the elements. These elements need to be connected to others, but not so rigidly that they can't also operate independently. Implicit in this adaptive model is the ability of a system to self-organize, which requires that its various component parts have coevolved through the presence of flexible network connections that facilitate communication and other adaptive relationships.[26]

The problem, of course, is that modern cities have few if any adaptive capacities. They are completely dependent on rapidly depleting energy sources, inefficiently distributed through an aging and highly centralized network of refineries and power plants. Countless forms of commodities and resources flow through cities, most of which are sourced from remote and often vulnerable locations and delivered via trucks on expensively maintained roadways. A heavy reliance on private automobiles results in a transportation monoculture that is prone to disruption and chronic inefficiencies, with the result that an estimated $115 billion is lost to the American economy each year because of traffic congestion, and $3.7 billion in Canada.[27] Modern deindustrialized cities fill highly specialized functions, most of which are unrelated to the manufacture and local distribution of necessary goods. Most serious of the many impediments to resiliency is that for the past two centuries cities have been built with an almost complete disregard for natural processes, with watercourses and prime farmland paved over and built upon with structures relying on air conditioning and gas heating to compensate for external environmental conditions.[28]

Major urban planning concepts have emerged over the past two decades under the rubric of a "sustainable cities" or "Smart Growth" agenda to redress these problems, which have become all too apparent after more than a half-century of rapid suburban expansion and automobile-oriented development. As a policy goal, a "sustainable cities" agenda has become fully integrated into urban planning and policy discourse, if not into actual urban outcomes. Despite being conceptualized and operationalized in terms of some generally recognized criteria as part of a vast literature, sustainable development resists universally accepted interpretations.

Meeting the demands of the three major dimensions of sustainable development—the ecological, economic, and social—presents many challenges, many of them political. Classical liberal political philosophy promotes the pursuit of individual liberty; and so, insofar as this depends on the consumption of resources, the ownership of land, and the ability to move about freely, there are perceived limits to what a democratic state may or should reasonably do to impose limits on such pursuits. As such, attempts to institutionalize sustainable development through Smart Growth initiatives have often been countered by social and fiscal conservatives and libertarians, on the grounds that such policies will stifle growth or pose unwarranted limitations on personal freedoms, and all in the name of addressing problems which in their view either aren't problems at all (e.g., there is no shortage of farmland) or are ideologically motivated.[29]

Contemporary measures to integrate Smart Growth in urban planning processes include encouraging a mix of housing types, rather than just single-family homes; investing in public transit systems such as bus rapid transit and light rail that can connect nodes more rapidly and efficiently; promoting "mixed use" developments that combine higher-density housing, shops, services, and amenities around public transportation routes (also known as "transit-oriented development" or TOD); "pedestrianizing" cities by improving "walkability" through well-designed pedestrian and cycling facilities that can enable people to more easily opt out of driving; focusing on infill opportunities such as those on former industrial lands; establishing greenbelts to protect farmland and natural areas; and instituting a suite of incentives, disincentives, and regulatory regimes to make it easier and more attractive for developers to create these patterns of development, rather than conventional, sprawling development. These urban forms reflect the resiliency value of diversity quite significantly by eschewing narrowly defined monocultural and industrial efficiencies of the sort that for so long enabled freeways and mass-produced suburban housing.

Strategies for mixing uses, increasing housing density, improving transit, and increasing options for nonmotorized transportation are not only essential for reducing energy consumption, but also offer city dwellers more choices in terms of where and how to live and how to get around. Compact and walkable developments become magnets for all kinds of desirable amenities such as street cafes, shops, and arts-related activities. While this program of development (or elements of it in various combinations) has been successfully sold as "New Urbanism" in both the United States and Canada, these approaches are, of course, a return to much older patterns of city building. They contribute to more humane urban environments, in which informal encounters between residents and shoppers are frequent, and opportunities for social connections and cohesion are integrated at all scales. The contemporary urban designer Jan Gehl calls these sorts of development "cities for people," which is really the ideal to which any city can aspire.[30]

As a major institution in the public realm, a key destination in which countless social interactions occur on a daily basis, and a primary "place" in any community, the public library can become a key player in such developments, as has indeed been the case in such places as Plainsboro, New Jersey, where its new public library became the focal point for a New Urbanist development, or in Seattle, where Rem Koolhaas's iconic design for its central library helped encourage a wave of ambitious downtown library redevelopment. As Shannon Mattern observes,

> All over the country, public library design projects are rallying communities around them, and the finished buildings are proving themselves beloved community gathering places. These are without question among the most vibrant public spaces in American cities today.[31]

Being community nodes and trip generators, public libraries are ideal anchor institutions in transit-oriented developments, as well as prime locations for cycling infrastructure. When colocated with other community amenities, they can help meet multiple needs and promote "trip-chaining" to reduce vehicle traffic. High design standards in library architecture and landscaping can support placemaking efforts, and library parks, plazas, and meeting rooms afford members of the public valuable public spaces. From Andrew Carnegie's day to our own, public libraries have always had a significant place in the city and as a force for urban development. Yet as important as they are, urban form considerations are not all that the public library can contribute to a resilient city.

Urban resilience and the public library

As we have seen above, terms such as *resilience* and *sustainable development* resist easy definition and prove contentious when applied to policy decisions. In an effort to more effectively operationalize the term *resilience*, Graeme Cumming and his colleagues sought in a 2005 paper to identify empirically measurable components that could contribute to the resilience of a socio-ecological system. In their view, a system's *identity* is the primary consideration, rather than merely its functions; and to support its continuance in the face of internal change and external shocks and disturbances, the identity of a system is supported by

- the components of the system;
- their interrelationships;
- sources of innovation; and
- sources of continuity across space and time.[32]

Significantly, Cumming et al. viewed continuity in terms of "system memory, which may take the form of elderly people, seed banks, social and biological legacies that remain after disturbances, customs and taboos, laws, or formal archives and libraries that become repositories of knowledge and also of identity."[33] For our purposes then, we can view the public library as an essential component of a community's "system memory," and one that assists the community in maintaining its identity and retaining access to local knowledge and history.

At a basic level the public library is a fundamental component of the public realm, along with the school system and other public services, and should ideally play a key role in assisting users in navigating the relationships between those components. The public library also fosters a community's learning capacity, by affording the opportunity for individuals and groups to gain new knowledge, create needed innovations, and forge new connections between social actors. Those libraries operating in metropolitan or regional systems fulfill a basic requirement for resilience through their distributed and redundant resources, rather than concentrating materials in one—potentially vulnerable—location. Each library provides a neighborhood reference point and is a memorable place; and many municipalities have sought to reinforce their urban identities through architecturally significant buildings.[34] Civic identity has always been expressed through memorable buildings and urban design, and this was certainly the case with Andrew Carnegie's program of public library building. In these ways, the roles and functions of the public library are quite consistent with the concept of resilience through the support of a system's identity.

Library practitioners, policy makers, and theorists have long made the connection between the "system identity" that is the city and the roles and functions of the public library. Born of the progressive beliefs in the positive and ameliorative effects of public interventions in social conditions, as well as in the ability of knowledge to elevate the individual and instill normative values, the modern public library has always been seen as more than another public service. It has been associated—at least by its advocates—with a faith in its power to yield broader social, economic, and cultural outcomes in society. As long ago as 1921, librarian and educator Arthur Bostwick would write in *The Library and Society* that

> the public library is destined to play an important part, to exercise an incalculable influence in the solution of the social problems of to-day. . . . The wisdom needed for this task is not to be found in schools or colleges but from the higher education of mature minds—the masses of the people—which the public library alone can give.[35]

While its initial missions may have been connected more with instilling middle-class values among surging immigrant populations, the public library's increasingly complex relationship with surrounding neighborhoods and the larger metropolitan context became apparent as North American cities grew rapidly following the Second World War. Librarians and municipal leaders alike began to wonder: what roles do and should public libraries fill in the modern city, and how should these roles change as cities themselves have changed?

The first systematic examination of this relationship was undertaken as a part of the Public Library Inquiry (1947–52) conducted by the Social Science Research Council at the request of the American Library Association (ALA). Rather than carrying out an internal (and potentially biased) review, the ALA sought the impartial observations of trained social scientists, in the hope that the findings would bolster their own professional assumptions about the value of the public library and thereby provide an empirical basis for their own lobbying efforts. To the dismay of many partisans, the inquiry concluded that the public library was not, in fact, meeting the demands of the masses but rather of a more educated stratum of society.[36]

With the rapid demographic, spatial, and economic shifts in the postwar era, public library administrators and city managers were forced to acknowledge that service models from earlier in the century were no longer commensurate with the forces at work in the contemporary American city. At a three-day symposium in 1963 on "Library Functions in the Changing Metropolis," librarians, administrators, planners, scholars, and political scientists gathered in Dedham, Massachusetts, to consider the changing metropolis: the demographic and financial implications of the rapid abandonment of traditional urban areas for the suburbs on the part of a white, middle-class, and print-oriented public, and what these trends would mean for library services. In the resulting volume, *The Public Library and the City*, the editor Ralph Conant asked:

> Libraries have . . . been one of the places where the talented of the lower classes have learned middle-class values. What role should the public library play in acculturation and education of low income groups who suffer economic deprivation because of functional illiteracy? Will the great central institution gradually be dismantled and even abandoned . . . [to deal with] the demand of outward moving middle classes . . . [through the] spatial dispersion of library facilities? [37]

Interestingly—and consistent with the modernist and utilitarian worldview dominating both urban planning and library thought at the time—the symposium also (uncritically) noted that

> [the urban] planner views the public library as an institution that should achieve publicly desirable goals and should be planned so as to achieve these goals with a maximum number of desirable consequences, a minimum number of undesirable ones, and at the lowest possible cost.[38]

The perennial debate over prescriptive vs. demand-based collection development (i.e., "good" books as opposed to popular fiction) was, as such, framed in terms of community planning outcomes: that "a library that is not used sufficiently is a waste of resources even if its goals are noble."[39] Accordingly, the contributors to the symposium focused on how to serve cost-effectively both a dispersed (mostly white and suburban) middle class as well as increasingly ghettoized African American populations. The very complexity of American metropolitan areas argued against any sort of hard-and-fast formula. This meant that each library must be planned according to an empirical assessment of the populations in their respective service areas:

> In middle class areas the contemporary library is desirable, with its
> emphasis on child student and nonfiction readers. In low income areas
> . . . the middle class library is unsatisfactory. Here a library is needed
> that invites rather than rejects the poorly educated. It should be geared
> to two types of readers: the small number who are already motivated,
> and may even have the middle-class values and skills that are prerequi-
> sites to using the library . . . [and those who] would like to read but are
> afraid or scornful of the ethos of the middle class library.[40]

This awareness grew throughout the 1960s to a more focused attention on the crisis in America's cities. As Kathleen de la Peña McCook (2001) recounts, public libraries received funding from President Johnson's War on Poverty programs, and the ALA in 1968 created its Coordinating Committee on Service to the Disadvantaged and held the first meeting of the Social Responsibilities Round Table the following year.[41] The need to better respond to growing social needs in that era also led to the widespread development of community information collections that indexed and linked patrons with social services.[42] In 1990, the ALA Council endorsed a "Library Services for Poor People"; while some critics like Sanford Berman have pointed out that the policy has been inadequately promoted and unevenly implemented in the intervening years, rapidly changing economic realities in the United States are compelling public libraries to provide more attention to low-income clientele.[43, 44] A remarkable example of this is the San Francisco Public Library, which has hired a professional social worker to provide visitors in need with referrals to social services.[45]

The ability of public libraries to address the needs of diverse urban users is inherent in their structure. In a 2009 paper, geographers Ruth Fincher and Kurt Iveson found that public libraries are a form of urban infrastructure that does not merely embrace diversity but helps to distinguish different kinds of diversity. Specifically, they observe that there are three social phenomena in cities that affect the ability of an individual or group of individuals to access a city's services: wealth and poverty; social status; and what they refer to as "hybridity," or the antiessentialist recognition that individuals are complex and can't be defined and limited by any classification. The public library, they write, negotiates these social realities through redistribution, recognition, and encounter.[46]

Just as much urban planning is inherently redistributive, in that it seeks to reduce to the extent possible locational disadvantage by distributing urban assets across the city, Fincher and Iveson point out that public library branches are situated so as to increase the potential for users of all incomes to access them. However, this redistribution isn't enough: giving people a right to urban amenities doesn't mean they will feel free to access them if they feel they don't "fit in" as a result of social stigma and denigration. This requires, they argue, the act of *recognition*, or the acknowledgment that certain classes of people have been subject to discriminatory cultural forces that have prevented them from full participation in society. There is an important distinction the authors make here that such recognition on the part of the public library shouldn't be merely affirmative but relational; that is, confirming the identity of a person within a particular social classification (e.g., African American) is not nearly as important as doing so within a context that has some bearing on the *relational* dimensions of these classifications. In other words, library programs and services should recognize the extent to which structural barriers and negative cultural patterns can affect a person or group of people based on potential social classifications. Determining if users are restricted in their freedom to use the library based on status relations, write Fincher and Iveson, is much more important than affirming social identities.[47]

The third dimension identified by Fincher and Iveson is perhaps the most affirming of the public library's identity and purpose: that of encounter. They argue that the goal of both urban planning and public libraries is not to let people "be themselves"—and thus remain fixed within social categories—but rather, through encounters with other people, to develop new social relations and through them develop new identities. The contribution that public libraries can make in this exploration, they stress, is that, unlike any other public space in which people may gather, the level and type of conviviality required for these interpersonal transformations are facilitated by the library through its collections and services. A public realm alone is not enough:

> To step into a public library is to step into a space that is shared with "strangers," in the form of other library users and library staff. As such, the forms of encounter that might occur between these strangers are mediated by the normative expectations about how a library should be used that are extant in any given library. . . . One of the remarkable features of "library-ness" most commonly identified in research on contemporary public libraries concerns the diversity of uses and users that libraries can accommodate. Reading newspapers, checking community notices, checking email, surfing the Internet, doing homework, relaxing with a coffee, attending lectures and community meetings, listening to live or recorded music, discussing a book with staff or other users, flirting, meeting and making friends. . . . All of these encounters are significant. They are premised on the capacity of those who use the library to mutually negotiate their common status as library users in

the moments of their encounters. This is a process of mutual (if temporary) identification which transcends fixed identity categories.[48]

Such encounters within the library can contribute to community-building, as
can the many services through which these encounters occur. However, as McCook
(2000) showed, while public libraries and librarians have long engaged in a broad
range of activities supporting the development of their communities, they have
been less proactive in putting themselves "at the table" of community planning
efforts.[49] More recently, however, the Urban Libraries Council (ULC) has documented the extensive work being done in Chicago in engaging their communities
by recognizing and building on existing assets and relationships between individuals and their institutions.[50] Numerous cases cited by the ULC demonstrate
how public library collections and services can, as "place-based assets," enhance
and strengthen economic development and revitalization efforts.[51] Furthermore,
many public libraries have joined in the efforts to build sustainable communities. As Kathryn Miller found in her 2010 book, public libraries are going "green"
through energy-efficient building practices, reducing water consumption, green
procurement, a shift away from the use of toxic chemicals in their buildings, and
fulfilling environmental education goals through programming.[52] She suggests,

> Environmental leadership and education are growth opportunities for
> the twenty-first century public library . . . Environmental education is
> yet another way the public library can help its community take another
> step towards societal progress.[53]

For all the potency or effectiveness of these diverse missions, though, it
remains problematic that public libraries in the United States have no unifying,
national mission. Each public library defines its own mission and tailors it to the
library's respective community, and while this may afford benefits for those communities, Glen Holt counters that this is also the public library's greatest weakness: without a statement of their national importance, there is, as a consequence,
no commensurate national mandate or funding.[54]

Such a national mandate would, unfortunately, bring with it a significant
political dimension, and the requisite need to navigate and contend with the
divisiveness that has always characterized America's political culture. In his 2001
manifesto, *Civic Librarianship*, Ronald McCabe views public libraries within the
context of America's "cultural civil war" between the forces of liberalism and lib-
ertarianism. He argues for a return to civic librarianship that can inform and
participate in the "community movement," the characteristics of which include

> discovering social and political common ground; renewing a social
> morality that balances rights and responsibilities; collaborating to solve
> social problems; strengthening institutions and civil society; reexam-
> ining zoning laws and community planning to enhance civic life.[55]

According to McCabe, the foundation of the culture wars is the tension
between the empiricism of the Enlightenment and the reaction of Romanticism,

which rebelled against the notion that there is one truth, one commonly agreed-upon structure of the world which can be revealed through objective study. Taken to its extreme, he argues, Romanticism becomes anti-intellectual, anti-social, anti-education, and hyper-individualistic, for it supposes that humans can and should exist in their purist form untainted by civilization and without reference to common understandings and consensual approaches to the running of a civil society—essentially a denial that a society should be built on shared knowledge.[56]

McCabe sees a linkage between the New Left's reaction against the state born of a rejection of war and unjust social policies, and that inherited by the New Right in the 1980s in their own attacks on the interventionist state. The boundaries in American political life have thus grown more pronounced. As discussed above with regard to urban development, libertarians are consistently opposed to governmental authority and control over one's life, be it economic or social. Liberals, meanwhile, are statist on socioeconomic issues but libertarian on moral ones; conservatives the opposite. Yet, what should be seen as positions on a continuum are instead, in McCabe's view, positioned as "false choices . . . between anarchy and authoritarianism in the life of society and between relativism and absolutism in the intellectual life."[57] McCabe doesn't necessarily blame the withdrawal of public life (as documented by Robert Putnam in his book *Bowling Alone*) as a result of countercultural and libertarian thought, but stresses that these philosophies validated these trends in the mind of the public. The response of what McCabe refers to as the "community movement" is to seek balance between the extremes of social conservatives and individualists. No group can impose their will on a pluralistic society; at the same time, no society can function as a collection of atomized individuals who share no social norms or are incapable of engaging in dialogue. In this regard McCabe echoes Bostwick, who in *The Library and Society* (1921) noted,

> Those who think on this subject and who really desire the improvement of society . . . are divided over the question whether mankind shall progress by the path of individualism or that of collectivism. Extremists assure us that these paths go in opposite directions, or traverse each other at right angles. The truth is they run parallel; and we have been travelling both, now advancing more on one and then on the other, towards the ultimate goal of humanity—the perfection of society through the elevation of the individual, the perfection of the individual through the improvement of society. Each helps the other; neither can be independent of the other.[58]

Interestingly, McCabe identifies mainstream public library services as distinctly libertarian. Where the public library movement in the United States has its roots in the Enlightenment view on progress and the perfectibility of mankind, in the wake of cultural civil war of 1960s, what had been an attempt to balance individual enlightenment and an informed citizenry was replaced in the 1980s with a focus on the autonomy of individuals. This happened to appease both the expressive individualism of the left and the utilitarian individualism on the right. The result for McCabe, however, is that public libraries have put themselves in the position of educating without actually educating, and cites the example of the 1980 American Library Association report *Planning Process for Public Libraries,* which assumed that libraries do not lead communities but that communities determine what kind of libraries they need. Libraries therefore can't be evaluated by an external standard. The public library is as a consequence required to shift from education to merely providing information, leaving it to the individual to determine what to do with that information. The effect, McCabe argues, has been crippling:

> The new institution no longer claimed to overtly educate the community, no longer claimed to prescribe specific social outcomes. Librarians and trustees . . . were no longer confident in their ability to understand the world; they no longer believed in the right to exercise the social authority of educators and community leaders. This led to a shift in the missions of the institutions from education for a democratic society to the more utilitarian mission of providing access to information for individuals.[59]

Absent a broader social mission, McCabe warns, the public library has no moral foundation and stands for purely utilitarian goals, an amoral component of the marketplace.[60]

This also parallels the postwar trajectory of urban planning. Demoralized and delegitimized as a result of both disastrous early postwar planning (such as freeway construction and dehumanizing public housing projects) and the brilliant assault on its hubristic excesses by Jane Jacobs in her 1961 classic *The Death and Life of Great American Cities*, planning largely retreated from any pretense of societal leadership and assumed a largely reactive stance, essentially as an adjunct of the development industry. In a 2011 essay on the legacy of Jacobs, planning scholar Thomas Campanella writes,

> [Jacobs's critique] diminished the disciplinary identity of planning. . . . And once the traditional focus of physical planning was lost, the profession was effectively without a keel. It became fragmented and balkanized, which has since created a kind of chronic identity crisis—a nagging uncertainty about purpose and relevance. . . . We have become a caretaker profession—reactive rather than proactive, corrective instead of preemptive, rule bound and hamstrung and anything but visionary . . . We are entering the uncharted waters of global urbanization on a scale never seen. And we are not in the wheelhouse, let alone steering the ship. We may not even be on board.[61]

In the case of planning, Campanella warns that urban development processes can all too easily be derailed by a culture of pluralism, hyperindividualism, and relativism, where all views are seen to be equally valid. Similarly, Ronald McCabe believes that, without a moral claim for public libraries, the yardstick for their success is that they are used and therefore justify public support. The dilemma about this transformation (which McCabe stresses is not yet complete) is that the public library has become a social institution premised on unbounded individualism rather than collective interests.

The alternative for McCabe is a public library based on the emergent community movement that seeks to balance individual aspirations with a recognition that we are all members of a larger society to which and for which we have responsibilities. While McCabe's efforts to conflate the right's authoritarian turn and the left's pluralistic relativism are not entirely convincing, his principal contention is paramount to the objectives of this book: that public libraries should move from a libertarian model in which they are primarily a distributor of materials and services to a communitarian one in which the public library assumes a leadership role in addressing the needs of contemporary urban society through the distribution of materials and provision of services.[62]

For Kathleen de la Peña McCook, the public library must also be more engaged than it has been. In her 2000 book *A Place at the Table* she points out that public libraries have been largely absent from community planning processes, and have themselves been neglected by those leading these efforts, such as the New Urbanists. Seen as necessary but essentially passive institutions, public libraries, she argues, must be much more proactive about inserting themselves into community visioning exercises and—literally—placing themselves at the table whenever civic-minded organizations gather. As it stands,

> [public] library services . . . are not well understood by community-building organizations . . . [and] librarians have not been integrally involved with community visioning efforts and thus have not been identified as part of the comprehensive community-building strategies being developed today. The lack of librarian participants among the rosters of community visioning projects means that the library message is not being received.[63]

McCook finds this is a "puzzling situation," as her analysis of the community-building work with which public libraries are already engaged—from arts and culture, to local economic development, to employment training, family services, and welfare—"would, by any definition, be counted as substantive community-building activity."[64]

Glen Holt would likely argue that this absence is in part owed, again, to the lack of any unified policy or financial support from the federal government. The closest proxy, he notes, is that provided by the Urban Libraries Council, to "Strengthen the Public Library as an Essential Part of Urban Life."[65] Since 1971, the Urban Libraries Council has provided institutional and advocacy support for North America's public libraries in helping them serve the needs of their cities and has been recognized for this role. In its 2005 publication *The Engaged Library* the ULC offered not only examples drawn from Chicago for how public libraries can connect with their cities, but offered a "toolkit" that illustrates many of McCabe's and McCook's points: it aids libraries in identifying potential linkages with other institutions and associations, as well as community assets such as public spaces and community leaders. The final diagram in the report boldly situates the library in the center, with a host of community elements, assets, and attributes arrayed around it, with arrows in each case drawn in both directions, revealing the library to be the focal point of transactions of all kinds.[66] It is important that these relations are bidirectional, for they connote mutual benefit. The library may be a "magnet," but it is not the only center of gravity in a city, just as no city draws all resources and assets to itself. Each has drawing power, but these powers may only be augmented through the power of their relations with others.

It is these relations that permit the proactive stance advocated by Holt, McCabe, and McCook. It is not enough that the public library remain a mere vessel from which users can draw information as they see fit, nor to limit itself to offering spaces in which democratic processes may transpire according to the desires of participants, whomever they may be. The challenges of the twenty-first century are going to require the public library to actually insert itself into the democratic process, to adopt—as McCabe would have it—"civic librarianship that seeks to strengthen communities through developmental strategies that renew the public library's mission of education for a democratic society."[67]

Thinning the container, strengthening the magnet

It is in the realm of democracy that the library and the city—and their attendant professions of librarianship and city planning—are connected most intimately. The mission of the public library movement has always been associated with providing access to information so as to encourage an informed citizenry and thus a healthy democracy. Molz and Dain (1999) state:

> Hallmark of a democratic society, the public library is an open, community-based institution ensuring the public's right to know, a defender of the free and open mind. Libraries remain complex, democratic, one-stop shopping and consultation centers for all manner of free (or mostly free) information, learning, cultural enrichment and entertainment for people of all ages and persuasions . . . as physical and intellectual presences they retain powerful symbolic as well as utilitarian importance in American Society.[68]

Primary among the public library's function in this regard is its ability to provide what Ray Oldenburg calls a "third place," a public gathering spot away from home and work where people can engage in meetings both informal and formal—and such places are in short supply in an increasingly privatizing world, where shopping malls can provide only the barest facsimile of a public realm.[69] This is why Jay Walljasper grants such prominent place to libraries—and the information commons—in his book *All That We Share: A Field Guide to the Commons*. For Walljasper, the library is a prime example of the "commons"—an idea around which all communities were once based but is now both unusual and under siege through existing and sought corporate ownerships. The commons is that which we hold in common—natural elements such as air and water but also physical places within the city such as parks, sidewalks, and libraries. It is also made up of our socio-technological artifacts such as the airwaves, the Internet, and Wikipedia.[70] The library, as a physical repository for information as well as a place for sharing it, becomes not just a part of the information commons, but the bridge between this intangible commons and that of the city itself.

In the city we see the location of the more traditional commons of streets and squares where free assembly is guaranteed, where institutions of democratic processes are concentrated, and where social categories are expressed spatially, even if they remain unacknowledged. Truly public spaces offer the possibility of multiplying the efforts of individuals to motivate and institute transformational shifts in governance and policy changes challenging these categories. In the wake of the 2011 "Arab Spring," particular attention was directed by urbanists to the fact that these events transpired in ancient cities with real and vital public spaces such as Cairo's Tahrir Square—and that the public realm had made these revolutions possible in a way that social media alone never could have.[71]

The professional planner, in seeking to effect incremental or dramatic transformation in spatial and social arrangements, must engage political actors within the accepted conventions of democracy—which, in their turn, public libraries nourish and defend. The city and the library can also be said to be related structurally, in the sense that they are spatially organized through zoning and classification, and indexed via cataloging and street coordinates, all in an effort to, as Alberto Manguel has it, contain the uncontainable through an imposed "vision of the world."[72]

For here we come to the most germane of all these interrelationships and shared commitments: the city and the public library are both at once containers and magnets. In his classic book *The City in History*, Lewis Mumford identified the origin of human settlements in the various forms of storage containers that allowed people to accumulate and organize surplus goods, and the city itself would become humanity's greatest container. In becoming the focal point for surplus, as well as for the organized hierarchical societies designed to organize and distribute this surplus, the city would also become a magnet that would draw people and economic activities from broad regions. Over time, he wrote, as societies and their technologies, literature, culture, and civilizations became more sophisticated, the container of the city (most coherently expressed in its massive external walls) became thinner, and eventually became—in the words of historian Arnold Toynbee—"etherealized" or dematerialized, rendered intangible or symbolic. Walls give way to recognized convention and lines on maps, even as the power of the urban magnet grows. Mumford saw that the dynamic between etherealization and magnetism was a constant in urban societies, and in the closing pages muses on what he called the "invisible city"—the emerging potentialities of telecommunications and the distributed interconnections of resources around the globe.[73]

The Internet age has permitted the etherealization of the city in ways that Mumford could never have imagined. Employment, services, shopping, entertainment, and recreation can now all be had online, and people can work from anywhere. However, where some early observers saw in these trends an end of the need for cities, quite the reverse has happened. As Frances Cairncross predicted in her 2001 book *The Death of Distance*, cities and urbanity have actually taken on a new importance in the digital age, as magnets for culture, recreation, and creativity.[74] This is a major thread of the whole "creative class" argument in urban planning and economics articulated by Richard Florida—that those cities that will thrive in the twenty-first century will be those best able to provide a high quality of life for creative workers, in the form of amenities, street life, and cultural infrastructure—including public libraries.[75] As the container is thinned, the magnet has grown more powerful. In his 2011 book *The Triumph of the City*, Edward Glaeser suggests that this shouldn't surprise us: after all, he writes,

> a few decades of high technology can't trump millions of years of evolution. Connecting in cyberspace will never be the same as sharing a meal or a smile or a kiss. . . . The most important communications still take place in person, and electronic access is no substitute for being at the geographic center of an intellectual movement.[76]

In other words, the role of—and demand for—great urban spaces has only grown in the Internet age. This has been particularly the case where public libraries are concerned. Far from being rendered obsolete by the digital age, the public library—once seen only as a "container" of paper documents—has become even more of a magnet for users, who have flocked to gain access to public workstations for Internet access, particularly with the onset of the current recession. Indeed, as Shannon Mattern notes,

> A number of new public library buildings have played significant roles in downtown revitalization projects, and they have helped cities— many in a stage of transition during the 1990s, as these libraries were coming into being—to redefine their civic identities. In short . . . urban public library buildings have loudly and convincingly reassured their relevance in this age of informational and urban sprawl. They are potent forces in giving shape and character to both the urban and the information environments.[77]

According to a 2010 report by the Institute for Museum and Library Services, nearly a third of the U.S. population over fourteen used their public libraries to access the Internet; and it is now among the most sought-after public library services.[78] As the recession surged in 2009 public library circulations in the United States were up 6 percent, many of them seeking assistance with job searches.[79] The importance of facilitating Internet use was highlighted in May 2011 when Frank LaRue, the special rapporteur on the promotion and protection of the right to freedom of opinion and expression for the United Nations, submitted a report indicating that access to the Internet—and more particularly the physical infrastructure that makes it possible—was a human right, as it is a key element in our ability to communicate and express ourselves.[80]

Once merely at the service of their neighborhoods and cities, public libraries are now connected to every other library and to the global library of data, media, information, and opinion stored on the Internet. Every aspect of information provision has been etherealized. Books are increasingly being read in digital form: by mid-2010 Amazon reported that e-books outsold hardcovers, while in the last three months of that year they outsold paperbacks.[81, 82] Reference services have been largely "disintermediated" by Google, to the extent that the company's name has become a verb synonymous with searching for information. Public libraries are even "loaning" e-books, although the business model is still being worked out, with publishers wanting libraries to repurchase rights to e-titles after a certain number of "circulations."[83] The façade of this "etherealized" library, wrote William Mitchell in his *City of Bits*,

> is not to be constructed of stone and located on a street in Bloomsbury, but of pixels on thousands of screens scattered throughout the world. . . . Reading tables become display windows on screen . . . the huge stacks shrink to almost negligible size, the seats and carrels disperse, and there is nothing left to put a grand façade on.[84]

The relationship between the library and the user has, appropriately, changed as citizens become "prosumers" that both produce information in the form of tweets, blog entries, and YouTube videos, and consume it on an ever-more portable array of devices. With the installation of wireless hotspots in public spaces (including, of course, libraries themselves) and 3G and 4G networks servicing smartphones, iPads, and other tablets, "the library" has become etherealized to the point where each of us can now access more information in our smartphones than anyone could hope to read in a hundred lifetimes. For Alberto Manguel, writing in *The Library at Night,* the Enlightenment vision of a "world encyclopedia, the universal library, exists, and is the world itself."[85] James Gleick, too, notes in his 2011 book *The Information* that the world has in essence become a "Library of Babel" and all of us are its librarians.[86]

But just as the physical commons were once enclosed and the public spaces in cities are largely privately owned (such as coffee shops), so too is the Internet commons under threat of enclosure. What is known as "Net neutrality"—the unfettered and free Web through which any website may appear on a list of results based on the search terms used—is being challenged around the world by large telecommunication corporations seeking the ability to charge for premium access to the Web, as well as those who would like to restrict access to certain sites on ideological, political, and "security" grounds. Under the privatized, "tiered" Web model being promoted by the telecom companies, some could pay for the privilege of greater access to the Web and to dominate search results, while smaller, less endowed organizations could be crowded out. The passage in the United States of the Federal Communication Commission's Open Internet Order in December 2010, which mandated transparency on the part of Internet service providers and forbade blockage of lawful content as well as discrimination of access, has not quelled this debate; as of this writing, Republicans are vowing to overturn it. (In November 2011, the Senate voted to reject Republican opposition to the FCC rules in support of neutrality announced in September, although several telecommunications corporations, including AT&T Verizon, are planning court challenges, which may be heard in 2013.) While there have long been debates over censorship in libraries, their noncommercial nature as well as their institutional commitments and histories make similar prospects affecting libraries virtually unthinkable.

Yet, for all our access to "free" information and our pretensions of living in an "Information Age," it is apparent that we are, ironically, actually living in a shockingly misinformed society. Studies and polls continually reveal that large minorities of Americans hold demonstrably false beliefs, not only about science (i.e., that the Earth is only thousands of years old) but about recent history (WMDs were discovered in Iraq), current events (President Barack Obama is a foreign-born Muslim), and their civic realm. Worse, studies also show that political partisans, when confronted with documented facts that contradict such beliefs, defend those beliefs even more adamantly.[87] The deterioration of political discourse has become such that, in April 2012, *Chicago Tribune* columnist Rex Huppke wrote a popular (and only somewhat tongue-in-cheek) obituary to Facts, in which our shared understandings of the world, after reeling from decades of such assaults as the Monica Lewinsky affair and President George W. Bush's justifications for the war in Iraq, finally succumbed. In it, he quotes Northwestern University sociology professor Gary Fines, who counters that, "facts aren't dead. If anything, there are too many of them out there. There has been a population explosion."[88] Which is precisely the problem: there may be exponentially more information available, but it has become commensurately more difficult to discern its provenance, quality, and appropriateness. In his book *Just How Stupid Are We?* (2010) Rick Shenkman observed that the delusions many Americans hold "can be traced to our mistaking unprecedented access to information with the actual consumption of it."[89]

None of this is to say that facts should not be contested; far from it. The act of challenging or refuting assumptions is a fundamental part of any democratic process. However, such counterarguments must themselves be defensible by reference to some external form of validation, be it empirical evidence, traditional knowledge, the precedent of literature, or a body of humanist ethics, not merely faith or opinion. This is why libraries have always been at the foundation of the intellectual life of any society that builds them, for they afford that society the opportunity to store, organize, refer to, and build upon such information for the present and into posterity. However, libraries are by definition more than merely accumulations of information; their curatorial function in the service of collection building lends rigor as well as transparency to the formation of collective memory.

The universal library of the Internet, by contrast, provides us opportunities for information consumption that beggar the imagination; the sheer volume of media channels, including cable, satellite, and web-based content represents an unprecedented information environment with which we are scarcely equipped to cope. As Bill McKibben demonstrated in his 1993 (and pre-Web) classic *The Age of Missing Information,* the ironic result of this bombardment of mass media is that our psyches have become polluted with inanities while the essential truths about how the natural world actually works have become almost unknown to us.[90] Without such moorings, our ability to distinguish the reasonable from the irrational appears to have become terminally crippled, and a whole range of opinions have arisen in the body politic that compete with one another—on the basis of evidence whose legitimacy no opponent will admit. In what is arguably among the most consequential of these cases is the "debate" on whether or not climate change is a hoax, furiously waged online even as swathes of Russia burned, parts of Australia drowned, and the American Midwest was torn apart by tornados. The extent of disinformation and misinformation on a wide range of essential issues—much of it officially sanctioned and promoted—prompted the organization Project Censored in 2010 to declare a "truth emergency," which they describe as

> the lack of purity in news brought about by . . . propaganda and distraction. It is the state in which people—despite potentially being awash in a sea of information—lack the power of discernment, creating a paucity of understanding about what it all means. In short, we are living in a time when people do not know whom to trust for accurate information and thus yearn for the truth. . . . So many critical subjects remain . . . unreported or so tightly wrapped in propaganda that they literally make no sense. Faced with accounts that aren't helping them understand or fix their deteriorating circumstances, people are growing angry and turning to other information sources, primarily on the Internet.[91]

This mass shift to online media is not without cost. There is growing evidence that the constant availability of online information simply isn't good for us or our social relationships. Studies are showing that Internet users who are continually tracking news are subject to constant stress, and even while our brains are processing and synthesizing all this new (and often distressing) data, those parts of the brain responsible for empathy and emotional intelligence remain inactive.[92] We may become intellectually stimulated by what we read, but remain unmoved even to the needs of those around us. Sherry Turkle writes in her 2010 book *Alone Together*, we have become so accustomed to the shallow, frequent, and decontextualized interactions on sites like Facebook and Twitter that our real-world relationships are suffering.[93] As two additional titles from 2010 confirmed, there is still much to debate about the Google era. Nicholas Carr's cautionary *The Shallows* argued that the Web is rewiring our brains and crippling our ability to concentrate, while Jaron Lanier's *You Are Not a Gadget* observed that the "hive mind" of the Web threatens our sense of individuality and of humanness itself.[94]

These phenomena are, of course, the complete antithesis of those associated with the experience of using a library. Where libraries concentrate our focus, invite contemplation, and increase social capacity through encounters and collaboration, the Web, by its very structure, encourages hyperindividuality and superficiality. Its reach in terms of potential collaboration may be unmatched, but the quality of these encounters remains open to debate. We must remember that the Web is a tool, and like any other may be overused, abused, or used inappropriately; the library, by contrast, is both a *place* and an institution, an "addiction" to which may pose a risk of mere eccentricity, rather than outright anomie.

This is one more reason why any talk of the Web replacing the library is not just shortsighted in the extreme but contrary to our needs as human beings, as social animals. It also—not incidentally—ignores the essential role that physical libraries can play in what must be a social, cultural, and political project of the first order: generating, communicating, and synthesizing the information needed to build the knowledge base commensurate with the multiplying and interrelated challenges of the twenty-first century. Without some mediating and curatorial force or institution to help bridge this chasm between the mass of information that is being produced and what is actually comprehended, a host of policy problems facing our society will have little hope of being assessed rationally. In his 2001 bestseller *The Demon-Haunted World,* Carl Sagan presciently wrote:

> I have a foreboding of an America in my children's or grandchildren's time—when the United States is a service and information economy; when nearly all the key manufacturing industries have slipped away into other countries; when awesome technological powers are in the hands of a very few, and no one representing the public interest can even grasp the issues; when the people have lost the ability to set their own agendas or knowledgeably question those in authority; when . . . our critical faculties in decline, unable to distinguish between what feels good and what's true, we slide, almost without noticing, back into superstition and darkness.[95]

Rather than being an Information Age, then, ours is perhaps in danger of becoming an Age of Ideology and Belief—for it is one in which our beliefs are vastly augmented by instantaneous access to the beliefs of others. Combined with unpredictable economic turmoil and the upending of long-held expectations about entitlement and privilege—that is to say, the trappings of the American Dream that are so essentially fixed to the suburban landscape—it is becoming ever more difficult to chart a feasible course through crisis, because we are apparently no longer capable of even agreeing on what the problems are. As author Danny Schechter notes, "the worse things get, the harder it is for people to agree on what to do."[96] In such a context, public policy decisions on a whole range of pressing social, environmental, and economic issues are being influenced or derailed altogether by debates governed by ideological preconceptions rather than by actual information. As a result, we slide ever further into seemingly intractable crises.

The public library and the "citysystem"

In such an environment—when reliable and diverse information about the issues facing society is as necessary as civilized, reasoned, and informed debate about those issues—the need for robust and engaged public libraries mandated with contributing to both would seem paramount. Robert Putnam puts it this way:

The prediction that the World Wide Web would kill libraries ignores another essential role of the public library in the Internet Age. The almost inconceivable variety of information available online is a mixed blessing. Finding a few needles of useful, reliable information in vast haystacks of junk calls for precisely the skills that librarians have always had. . . . The techno-utopian belief that access to unlimited information automatically translates into understanding and knowledge has proven to be false. Trained guides are more important than ever, and libraries provide them.[97]

It is important as well to recognize that this universe of information is but one of the resources, just one of the flows, that intersect the contemporary city:

The city is seen as a focal point for a wider complex of economic, social, political and environmental linkages and flows of power, energy and information. Because it is a focal point, place and context remain important as nodes through which power, energy and information flow and may be transformed. Indeed, it is contestation over patterns of distribution and transformation of these three flows that shape urban life.[98]

It is these transformative flows that Jeb Brugmann describes as an unfolding "urban revolution," a globally interconnected stream of resources and networks coalescing around the half of the world's people who live in cities. Key to what Brugmann terms a city's "urban advantage" are its density, scale, and ability to promote association and extension (i.e., networking and global reach). Here, too, the public library is perfectly situated to build, promote, and facilitate associations and connections, and to contribute to extensions of all kinds, be they virtual, entrepreneurial, or institutional. In the face of the challenges urban societies are facing, Brugmann calls for a "citysystem," an organic combination of spatial, economic, social, entrepreneurial, and political forces that express a community's "strategic ambitions" through "co-building" and resource/waste flows that are modeled on natural ecosystems.[99] Given these demands and potentialities, it would seem more important than ever that public libraries be capable of contributing to citysystems, and of engaging in the kind of multi-sectoral collaboration that would permit these sorts of extensions and associations. In its 2009 report, *The Engaged Library*, the Urban Libraries Council argued that public libraries are able to contribute to successful community building by

discovering and mobilizing layers of assets already present in every community [including] the skills and resources of its individuals, the power of relationships in voluntary associations, assets present in the array of local institutions, the physical infrastructure of the community, the profile and dynamics of the local economy, [as well as] the stories that define the community, its history and its dreams.[100]

But in this task the public library cannot—and is simply not capable—of acting alone. While the public library may indeed be seen by its publics as their "front porch," Michael Cart observes that

> the public library is more important than ever before as a centering institution, as a place of gathering, and as an equalizer, but the public library cannot build community by itself. The problems are simply too great. The library needs partners and it needs a place at the community planning, policy making, and development table. There needs to be collaborating and forming partnerships and alliances. If public libraries really want to have effective partnerships and make a difference in their communities they have to be part of the decision-making process in those communities. They have to be at the table with other organizations and government agencies. They have to be involved in giving and getting assets for the common good of the community.[101]

Such would seem to point to the need for a national public library strategy to make these interconnections possible. Yet, as Glen Holt points out, the very strength of public libraries as local institutions is also their greatest weakness: their localism and the constraining local nature of their funding base is matched by their lack of a national mandate or statement of purpose, which they need to fulfill their historic and newly emerging purposes.[102]

What follows in these pages will, I hope, assist in articulating why such a national mandate is desirable, and why any national urban strategy should include a commensurate, complementary, and equally robust public library strategy. While the chapters in this volume are mostly American, several are Canadian, one is European, and one is from Africa. They may each have their particular local contexts, but they also speak to the universal values of public libraries in any context.

Glen Holt begins the collection with a statement querying our assumptions about resiliency and the extent to which public libraries may be able to contribute to it, given the constrained environment in which they are presently situated. He rightly argues that the promotion of "resilience" cannot be a matter of faith, but must, like other purported library contributions to community well-being, be intentional and measurable. It can also, he stresses, be the result of services at which public libraries have always engaged.

This reality is demonstrated in case studies of public libraries addressing social issues through a familiar range of programs and services. Jennifer Hoyer considers how public libraries can combat social exclusion through collections and services, using the Atwater Library and Computer Centre (a Montreal subscription library) as an exemplar. Similarly, Vanessa Francis looks at the Enoch Pratt Library in Baltimore for examples of equitable services to address social needs. Queens Library demonstrates its own strengths in Deborah Olley Murphy and Denise Clark's examination of that library's "Literacy Zones." Finally, Monique Woroniak explains how outreach efforts on the part of the Winnipeg Public Library address the needs of two significant demographics in that city— Aboriginal people and newcomers in fiscally challenging circumstances.

There are, in addition, efforts at which public libraries are engaged that are nontraditional and also capable of generating significant impacts. Melissa Rauseo and Julie Edwards relate the collaborative efforts the public library led in Peabody, Massachusetts, to provide a free summer meal program for children and youth, while Mary Wilkins Jordan shows how public libraries can contribute to bringing the benefits of nature and green living things to urban areas through library gardens. The Urban Libraries Council discusses how public libraries and local governments can form "partnerships for the future" to build sustainable communities. An essential component of a sustainable, resilient city is that of "place," and Maija Berndtson reviews the significant achievements in library architecture that have made contributions to placemaking efforts, particularly in Europe.

These contributions describe the efforts of libraries in challenging times; yet libraries are also increasingly facing crisis. The director of the Houston Public Library, Dr. Rhea Lawson, and her colleagues Meller Langford and Roosevelt Weeks recount the harrowing days following Hurricane Ike, during which time the Houston Public Library provided invaluable service to America's fourth-largest city by offering its facilities and services to assist in disaster recovery. My colleague Matthew Evan Havens and myself then look ahead to the potential disruptions that an era of "peak oil" and climate change may bring to our cities, and how public libraries might be able to offer their support toward the necessary "transition" to a less energy-intensive future. The theme of crisis continues as Innocent Chirisa reveals the necessity of community leadership and collaboration efforts under conditions of severe financial privation in Harare, Zimbabwe—a sobering reminder of what is at stake for public libraries under austerity measures currently being considered by many governments around the world.

A powerfully recurring theme in these essays is that of partnership. All the efforts described cannot be undertaken by libraries alone, for they would strain already limited resources; this is why public libraries must reach out in new and powerful ways to their communities. In the concluding section, Pilar Martinez outlines the Edmonton Public Library's "community-led model" for service delivery, one which seeks to move beyond community participation and to empower communities to more significantly influence the direction of library collections and services.

I believe that these portraits of public libraries in action afford those of us who are passionate about libraries further confirmation of the vitality of the public library as a civic institution, and reveal to those professionally engaged in planning for cities that the public library can be a valuable ally in those efforts. With stressors on cities and their residents increasing almost daily, this book is a plea to preserving and defending the public library, or what Art Brodsky calls our "library lifeline;" for the resilience that our cities will need in a turbulent future may be found—at least in part—through its doors.

NOTES

1. Sue Halpern, "Mayor of Rust," *New York Times Magazine*, February 11, 2011, www.nytimes.com/2011/02/13/magazine/13Fetterman-t.html.

2. Levi Strauss Company, "Braddock Portraits: Episode 10. The Library," *We Are All Workers,* September 21, 2010, http://explore.levi.com/news/we-are-all-workers/.

3. Lewis Mumford, *The City in History: Its Origins, Its Transformations and Its Prospects* (New York: Harcourt, Brace and World, 1961).

4. Chris Turner, "The Ideal Urban Form," *Plan Canada* (Winter 2009): 48–51.

5. James Howard Kunstler, *The Geography of Nowhere: The Rise and Decline of America's Man-Made Landscape* (New York: Free, 1994).

6. Wendell Cox, *War on the Dream: How Anti-Sprawl Policy Threatens the Quality of Life* (New York: iUniverse, 2006).

7. Marylaine Block, *The Thriving Library: Successful Strategies for Challenging Times.* (Medford, NJ: Information Today, 2007).

8. Carl Grant, "How Librarians Can Shape the Future," *Public Library Quarterly* 29, no. 2 (2010): 96.

9. Gill Cooper and Genevieve Cooper, *Public Library Closures.* Knowledge and Information Management/Home Affairs Section, February 18, 2011 (London: House of Commons Library), www.parliament.uk/briefing-papers/SN05875.pdf.

10. Art Brodsky, "Our Public Library Lifeline Is Fraying. We'll Be Sorry When It Snaps," *Huffington Post,* April 11, 2010, www.huffingtonpost.com/art-brodsky/our -public-library-lifeli_b_533529.html.

11. Glen Holt, "Future Economic Realities for Libraries: Lessons from Current Events," *Public Library Quarterly* 28, no. 3 (2009): 250.

12. Alison Flood, "Chicago Commissioner Defends Library Funding," *Guardian,* July 8, 2010, www.guardian.co.uk/books/2010/jul/08/fox-news-libraries-chicago1.

13. John Nichols, "Learning the Fitzwalkerstan Way: Wisconsin's Walker Pushes Privatization of Education," *The Nation,* May 9, 2011, www.thenation.com/ blog/160518/learning-fitzwalkerstan-way-wisconsins-walker-pushes-privatization -education.

14. Henry Giroux, "Militarized Conservatism and the End(s) of Higher Education," *Truthout,* April 5, 2011, www.truth-out.org/militarized-conservatism-and-ends -higher-education#10.

15. United States Conference of Mayors, *2010 Hunger and Homelessness Survey: A Status Report on Hunger and Homelessness in America's Cities* (Washington, DC: City Policy Associates for the United States Council of Mayors, 2010).

16. Samuel Sherradon, "The Infrastructure Deficit," *The New America Foundation,* February 3, 2011, http://growth.newamerica.net/publications/policy/the _infrastructure_deficit.

17. Bjoern H. Amland, "Natural Disasters Displaced 42 Million Last Year," *Globe and Mail,* June 6, 2011, www.theglobeandmail.com/news/world/asia-pacific/natural -disasters-displaced-42-million-last-year/article2049669/.

18. Rachelle Alterman, *Planning in the Face of Crisis: Land Use, Housing and Mass Immigration in Israel* (London: Routledge, 2002).

19. Amy Goodman, "Naomi Klein: Why Climate Change Is So Threatening to Right-Wing Ideologues," *Alternet,* March 9, 2011, www.alternet.org/ environment/150180/naomi_klein%3A_why_climate_change_is_so_threatening _to_right-wing_ideologues/

20. Jeb Brugmann, *Welcome to the Urban Revolution: How Cities Are Changing the World* (London: Bloomsbury, 2009).

21. World Commission on Environment and Development, *Our Common Future* (New York: Oxford University Press, 1987), 43.

22. Andrew McMurray, "The Rhetoric of Resilience," *Alternatives* 36, no. 2 (Fall 2010): 22.

23. Lawrence J. Vale and Thomas J. Campanella, eds., *The Resilient City: How Modern Cities Recover from Disaster* (New York: Oxford University Press, 2005).

24. Peter Newman, Timothy Beatley, and Heather Boyer, *Resilient Cities: Responding to Peak Oil and Climate Change* (Washington, DC: Island, 2008).

25. Crawford S. Holling, "Resilience and Stability of Ecological Systems," *Annual Review of Ecology and Systematics* 4 (1973): 1–23.

26. Ibid.

27. David Schrank, Tim Lomax, and Shawn Turner, *2010 Urban Mobility Report* (College Station, TX: Texas Institute, 2010), http://tti.tamu.edu/documents/mobility_report_2010.pdf; Transport Canada, *The Cost of Urban Congestion in Canada* (Ottawa: Transport Canada, Environmental Affairs, 2006).

28. Michael Hough, *Cities and Natural Process: A Basis for Sustainability.* (New York: Routledge, 2004).

29. For more on these arguments, see Wendell Cox, *War on the Dream: How Anti-Sprawl Policy Threatens the Quality of Life* (New York: iUniverse, ca. 2006).

30. Jan Gehl, *Cities for People* (Washington, DC: Island, 2010).

31. Shannon Mattern, *The New Downtown Library: Designing with Communities* (Minneapolis: University of Minnesota Press, 2007), 41.

32. G. S. Cumming et al., "An Exploratory Framework for the Empirical Measurement of Resilience," *Ecosystems* 8 (2005): 975–87.

33. Ibid., 978.

34. Mattern, *The New Downtown Library.*

35. Arthur E. Bostwick, *The Library and Society* (Salem, NH: Ayer, 1977), 461.

36. Redmond Kathleen Molz and Phyllis Dain, *Civic Space, Cyberspace: The American Public Library in the Information Age* (Cambridge, MA: MIT Press, 1999), 16.

37. Ralph W. Conant, ed., *The Public Library and the City* (Cambridge, MA: MIT Press, 1965), 8.

38. Ibid, 67.

39. Ibid., 69.

40. Ibid., 71.

41. Kathleen de la Peña McCook, *A Place at the Table: Participating in Community Building* (Chicago: American Library Association, 2000).

42. Danielle P. Milam, "Access for All: Public Library Contributions to Civic Connectivity," *National Civic Review* 90, no. 3 (Fall 2001): 213–20.

43. Sanford Berman, "Classism in the Stacks: Libraries and Poverty," *Journal of Information Ethics* 16, no. 1 (Spring 2007): 103–10.

44. Leslie Edmonds Holt and Glen E. Holt, *Public Library Services for the Poor: Doing All We Can* (Chicago: American Library Association, 2010).

45. Charles London, "When Service Matters," *Library Journal* 135, no. 1 (January 2010): 40–43.

46. Ruth Fincher and Kurt Iveson, "Public Libraries in Cities of Diversity," paper delivered at the Australia Library and Information Association Summit, July 16, 2009.

47. Ibid.

48. Ibid., 8.

49. McCook, *A Place at the Table.*

50. Urban Libraries Council, *The Engaged Library: Chicago Stories of Community Building* (Chicago: Urban Libraries Council, 2007).

51. Roger L. Kemp and Marcia Trotta, *Museums, Libraries and Urban Vitality* (Jefferson, NC: McFarland, 2008).

52. Kathryn Miller, *Public Libraries Going Green* (Chicago: American Library Association, 2010).

53. Ibid, 2.

54. Glen Holt, "Future Economic Realities for Libraries, 249–68.

55. Ronald McCabe, *Civic Librarianship: Renewing the Social Mission of the Public Library* (Lanham, MD: Scarecrow, 2001), xiv.

56. Ibid., 6–7.

57. Ibid., 34.

58. Bostwick, *The Library and Society*, 458.

59. McCabe, *Civic Librarianship*, 35.

60. Ibid., 37.

61. Thomas Campanella, "Jane Jacobs and the Death and Life of American Planning," *Places: Design, Culture, Change*, April 25, 2011, http://places.designobserver.com/feature/jane-jacobs-and-the-death-and-life-of-american-planning/25188/.

62. McCabe, *Civic Librarianship*.

63. McCook, *A Place at the Table*, 40.

64. Ibid., 96.

65. Holt, "Future Economic Realities for Libraries," 260.

66. Urban Libraries Council, *The Engaged Library*.

67. McCabe, *Civic Librarianship*, 77.

68. Molz and Dain, *Civic Space, Cyberspace*, 185.

69. Ray Oldenburg, *The Great Good Place: Cafes, Coffee Shops, Bookstores, Bars, Hair Salons, and Other Hangouts at the Heart of a Community* (Cambridge, MA: Da Capo, 1999).

70. Jay Walljasper, *All That We Share: A Field Guide to the Commons* (New York: New Press, 2010), 7.

71. Josh Sanburn, "Square Roots: How Public Spaces Helped Mold Arab Spring." *Time Magazine*, May 17, 2011, www.time.com/time/world/article/0,8599,2071404,00.html.

72. Alberto Manguel, *The Library at Night* (Toronto: Alfred A. Knopf, 2006), 47.

73. Mumford, *The City in History*.

74. Frances Cairncross, *The Death of Distance: How the Communication Revolution Is Changing Our Lives*, rev. ed. (Boston: Harvard Business Press, 2001).

75. Richard Florida, *Cities and the Creative Class* (New York: Routledge, 2005).

76. Edward Glaser, *The Triumph of the City: How Our Greatest Invention Makes Us Richer, Smarter, Greener, Healthier, and Happier* (New York: Penguin, 2011), 248.

77. Mattern, *The New Downtown Library*, 37.

78. Samantha Becker et al., *Opportunity for All: How the American Public Benefits from Internet Access at U.S. Libraries* (Washington, DC: Institute of Museum and Library Services, 2010).

79. London, *When Service Matters*, 40.

80. Frank LaRue, "Report of the Special Rapporteur on the Promotion and Protection of the Right to Freedom of Opinion and Expression," United Nations General

Assembly, May 16, 2011, www.scribd.com/doc/56634085/Report-of-the-Special
-Rapporteur-on-the-promotion-and-protection-of-the-right-to-freedom-of
-opinion-and-expression-Frank-La-Rue.

81. Claire Cain Miller, "E-Books Top Hardcovers at Amazon," *New York Times,* July 19, 2010, www.nytimes.com/2010/07/20/technology/20kindle.html.

82. Emma Barnett, "Amazon Kindle E-Books Outsell Paperback," *Independent,* January 31, 2011, www.independent.ie/business/technology/amazon-kindle-ebooks -outsell-paperbacks-2517771.html.

83. Josh Hadro, "HarperCollins Puts 26 Loan Cap on Ebook Circulations," *Library Journal*, February 25, 2011, www.libraryjournal.com/lj/home/889452-264/ harpercollins_caps_loans_on_ebook.html.csp.

84. William Mitchell, *City of Bits: Space, Place and the Infobahn* (Cambridge, MA: MIT Press, 1996), 56.

85. Manguel, *The Library at Night,* 89.

86. James Gleick, *The Information: A History, a Theory, a Flood* (New York: Pantheon, 2011).

87. Joe Keohane, "How Facts Backfire," *The Boston Globe,* July 11, 2010, www.boston .com/bostonglobe/ideas/articles/2010/07/11/how_facts_backfire/?page=full.

88. Rex Huppke, "Facts, 360 B.C.–A.D. 2012: In Memoriam: After Years of Health Problems, Facts Has Finally Died," *Chicago Tribune*, April 19, 2012, www .chicagotribune.com/news/local/ct-talk-huppke-obit-facts-20120419,0,809470 .story.

89. Rick Shenkman, *Just How Stupid Are We?: Facing the Truth about the American Voter* (Memphis, TN: General Books), 2010.

90. Bill McKibben, *The Age of Missing Information* (New York: Random House, 1992).

91. Mickey Huff, Peter Phillips, and Kristina Borjesson, "Truth Emergency" and "Introduction," in *Censored 2011: The Top 25 Censored Stories of 2009–2010* (New York: Seven Stories, 2010).

92. Casey Miner, "This Is Your Brain on Change," *Ode* (June 2011): 28–32.

93. Sherry Turkle, *Alone Together: Why We Expect More from Technology and Less from Each Other* (New York: Basic Books, 2010).

94. Nicholas Carr, *The Shallows: What the Internet Is Doing to Our Brains* (New York: W. W. Norton, 2010); Jaron Lanier, *You Are Not a Gadget: A Manifesto* (New York: Knopf, 2010).

95. Carl Sagan, *The Demon-Haunted World: Science as a Candle in the Dark* (New York: Ballantine Books, 1997), 25.

96. Danny Schechter, "It Is 'March Madness' Time in the USA Where the Irrational Is Peddled as Rational, Provoking Intense Polarization and Paralysis," *CommonDreams,* March 6, 2011, www.commondreams.org/view/2011/03/06-0.

97. Robert D. Putnam and Lewis M. Feldstein, *Better Together: Restoring the American Community* (New York: Simon and Schuster, 2003), 48.

98. Mark Pelling, *The Vulnerability of Cities: Natural Disaster and Social Resilience* (London: Earthscan), 20.

99. Jeb Brugmann, *Welcome to the Urban Revolution*.

100. Urban Libraries Council, *The Engaged Library,* 3.

101. Michael Cart, "America's Front Porch—The Public Library," *Public Library Quarterly* 21, no. 1 (2003): 3–21.

102. Holt, "Future Economic Realities for Libraries."

chapter two

Dr. Glen Holt

Exploring public library contributions to urban resiliency

Resiliency is often viewed as the ability to recover from misfortune. The resilience of a city, town, or a village is demonstrated in its ability to regain lost status, restart economic development, or boost population growth in the face of challenging conditions.

Public libraries are not independent forces that automatically contribute to resilient cities. As a matter of faith, librarians and their supporters may believe their institutions have such inherent power. However, articles of faith, and the belief statements that are based on them, must not be confused with measured, direct impact or implied benefits inferred from logical analysis using established methodologies.

If we want our libraries to play a significant, documented role in contributing to urban resiliency, we need to define resiliency, illustrate how effective libraries add to resiliency, and suggest what can be done to help more libraries shift their expenditures and improve their services to play a significant role in contributing to the resiliency of their communities.

Resiliency: different and changing

Urban resiliency does not mean the same thing in Charlotte, Phoenix, or Detroit or a variety of communities large and small that host the 10,000 public library systems that exist in the United States. In each case the economic, cultural, and social situation is different. Library funding levels are different and institutional ideas of what constitutes good library service are often so different from one system to another that professional newcomers and first-time visitors react with shocked surprise when local staff reveal some rule or "usual practice." Moreover, massive external changes may cause dramatic downturns in conditions in some communities while raising others, in the process shifting the community definition of resiliency.

Here are some examples.

In 1950, St. Louis had 857,000 inhabitants. In 2000, it had 348,000. By 2008, the population of St. Louis had shown a small increase to 354,000.[1] The current mayor (in 2011) said that St. Louis was in resurgence because the city's claimed population was over 350,000. So, is St. Louis a resilient city? And if so, what made it resilient? And did the public library play a part?

In the census of 2000, New Orleans recorded 485,000 persons, down about 18 percent from a high twenty years earlier. In the years immediately after Hurricane Katrina and Hurricane Rita struck in 2005, New Orleans had 273,000 persons, 60 percent of its pre-disaster numbers. In 2008, the Census Bureau upped its estimate to 337,000, or 74 percent of the earlier population figure.[2] So is New Orleans a resilient city? And if so, what made it resilient? And did the public library play a part?

Then there is Abilene, Kansas, boyhood home of General and President Dwight David Eisenhower, which hosts his museum and presidential library, along with the Greyhound Hall of Fame and a few more mostly local attractions. Since 1950, the city of Abilene has added over a thousand persons, to reach 6,500 persons in 2000 but dropping to 6,300 inhabitants in 2010, a decline of 4.2 percent. In general, Abilene has higher family incomes, more jobs, and a more substantial "suburban growth" than at any time in its history.[3] So, is Abilene a resilient city? And if so, what made it resilient? And did the public library play a part?

To reiterate, a resilient place is one that can recover from misfortune. And, if you examine in much more detail St. Louis, New Orleans, or Abilene, you will find that to a greater or lesser degree these three all have made gains from relative stagnation or have come back from losses—of jobs, population, or from natural disasters—like hurricanes, floods, and shifting demographics and employment conditions. Moreover, all have experienced population shifts, as their inhabitants became wealthier or poorer or as new ethnic groups moved within or beyond their legal boundaries.

What role did the respective public libraries of these communities play in their relative resiliency over the last few decades?

Through St. Louis's half-century of decline, the St. Louis Public Library (SLPL) eked out its existence, closing branches, cutting staff, and savaging its materials budget, until the late 1980s, when its annual budget line in real dollars was just 42 percent of its late 1960s budget. In 1988 it won its first tax increase in decades, restoring the institution's purchasing power to late 1960s real-dollar levels. With new funds and a massive reorganization, the SLPL began to rebuild a position of prominence in its community. Before that resurgence, an examination of its input and output numbers suggests that this library system was doing little more than offering minimal services. By any but the loosest "contribution to urban resiliency" criteria, the SLPL was a minimal contributor to the civic landscape. From the late 1980s onward, as explained in later sections of this chapter, the library's board leadership and its administration became self-conscious about helping the city advance in many service areas critical to sustaining urban resiliency.

When Hurricanes Katrina and Rita struck New Orleans in 2005, its library system—like most of the state's libraries—was unprepared to deal with a disaster, minor or major. Responding to Katrina's devastation, the State Library, under its dynamic new leader, Rebecca Hamilton, made huge changes in the disaster-preparedness network for the state's libraries, and then proceeded to explain to the profession the steps forward even as reforms continued. When Hurricane Rita hit, many of the state's public libraries were ready. These facilities became disaster-recovery information centers, aiding out-of-towners in communicating with loved ones, and helping refugees in communicating appropriately with jobs and assistance agencies. Hamilton has made a very good case recently that many of the public libraries she watches over can and do contribute to community resiliency.[4]

The Abilene Public Library, housed in an old Carnegie building erected in 1904, and which expanded in 1977 and again in 2010 (this time paid for with a quarter-cent sales tax along with private-sector donations and bequests), has nine public-access computers. It is focused on community needs, especially those of children and teens, in the process building a strong traditional place and an electronic presence in the community. The library functions as a community center, offering a variety of activities for children and adults plus a wealth of information that helps visitors find their way to other attractions and services when they exit Interstate 70 to visit the Eisenhower Library or the Greyhound Hall of Fame. Just as importantly as its library-building place functions, the library plays a role as a virtual community meeting place, as evidenced by its Facebook page.[5]

Here then are just three exemplar libraries, each different, facing different external and internal issues. A case can be made that all three contribute or have contributed to the current resiliency of their communities. But the case is not easy to make, which has less to do with the libraries themselves than the state of statistical scholarship in the library profession.

If libraries want to have a positive impact on resilient cities, they must behave intentionally in that effort, and be capable of validating how well they are achieving the goals of this intentional work.

Intentioned library behavior

At the SLPL, for example, when the governing board decided the library needed to play a significant role in the city's positive developments, staff started by analyzing the community's needs. St. Louis's big problem was poverty, associated with low literacy and poor schools, composite and one-parent (usually female) households, parsimonious state expenditures for social services, and a declining or at least stagnant local tax base. Tied to these poverty statistics was a library reality: most poor, low-literate adults and children, many of the latter attending schools in the uncertified St. Louis public schools system, and most families without access to computers, saw the public library as contributing nothing to their family or job life. Available demographic and output statistics showed that the library was providing its services mostly to the city's middle-class families.[6]

The SLPL Board of Directors decided that the library ought to help the city's poor population. The first action was to reform the institutional mission statement to reflect new proactive concerns. Here is the mission and goals statement adopted in early 1994:

> The St. Louis Public Library will provide learning resources and information services that support and improve individual, family and community life. To support this mission, the library will organize and prudently manage its resources to:
>
> > Ensure that the library's resources are available to all;
> > Promote use of the library;
> > Assist children and adults with life-long learning;
> > Promote literacy for all ages;
> > Assist individuals in finding jobs and educational opportunities;
> > Assist businesses with their development and growth;
> > Provide current information;
> > Provide recreational reading resources, media materials, and programs;
> > Promote public use of modern information technology.[7]

For the library's role in helping make St. Louis more resilient, the critical word in the mission statement is "improve." When the Board of Directors inserted this word, it mandated the library to an *intentional* proactive role in helping sustain and enhance the community it served. Few public library mission statements carry this mandate to "improve" individuals, families, and the community. Few library mission statements carry such an explicit and implicit set of statements about how the library ought to behave to promote a resilient community. The SLPL mission statement is a declaration of intentionality.

Once the SLPL articulated this intentional mandate, staff developed a set of "talking points"—a little one-to-one model speech with which staff could tell individual users that the staff's job was helping them to meet their reading and research needs. Here was the "talking points" statement developed from that mission:

> We proactively help people, families, and the whole community to become better than they are now. When you visit the library, we start with where you are—your question, your inability to read, your lack of time, even the fact that you don't use the library—and we work to give you help to get you exactly the reading material or the information that you want or need to make your life better. We are in the business of helping you equip yourself to earn a living or to be an effective parent. What business would you have us be in other than helping you, your family, and your community? We do this work intentionally. We take our policy cues from you, our constituent taxpayers.[8]

To ensure that we were on cue in working with our constituents' and community's needs, we at the SLPL did lots of surveys and dozens of focus groups. In this process, we tried to take special care to obtain the voices of those who ordinarily did not speak up very much on matters of public policy. Our object was always the same: to enrich our intentional activities to make them meet needs while fitting within our articulated mission.

Intentionality is the imperative when libraries set out to play a significant role in the lives of their communities. Support for an intentional approach comes from within the computer programming community. It is articulated for that sector by the influential software designer Bjarne Stroustrup, who points out that all of us are dependent on software, but much of it is unreliable and inadequate for what it's used for. Stroustrup says the reason for this lack of customer personalization is the isolation of software writers who design for themselves, not for users. "Software that satisfies and delights is as rare as a phoenix," Stroustrup concludes.[9]

Like our own efforts at the SLPL, Stroustrup's remedy is to start by talking with users to find out what they want. Then, he says, design software intentionally rather than serendipitously to meet customer needs. Stroustrup states that designing software for customers is a "disruptive" process, but this intentionality is the only way to use the industry's real creative intelligence to bring about the neat, elegant packages that users actually want, rather than the bloated conglomerates that are accumulated when attempting to meet the needs of all people without considering the specific needs of any single person.[10]

In their misappropriated eagerness to follow the loud voice of retail marketing mavens, libraries often make the same kind of agglomerating error. The irrational library public relations cry that "this library has something for everyone" is as false as the purported scream of the extinct dodo bird. Thoughtful library leaders never make this claim.

To play a role in community resiliency, libraries need to thoughtfully and intentionally develop the significant library-based services that will serve the needs of their user communities.

Measurable results

We work in an age of accountability. The concept of accountability is hardly new; it has its U.S. origins in the world's religions. Through the fin de siècle of the nineteenth century, however, Americans, especially those engaged in the development of their reform-oriented professions, secularized accountability using statistics of many different kinds to become what historian Robert Bremner calls a "factual generation."[11] These reform groups generated statistical reports on all kinds of behavior and used facts, especially numerical facts, as a policy tool that soon came to pervade education, economics, political science, sociology, medicine, and the practice of social work.

In some disciplines—like education—many current statistical indicators, mostly measured by external experts and for political purposes, show the profession in a critical light. Examining the results of these trends in February 2011, educator Diane Ravich summarized the result:

> So long as educational decisions continue to be made not by seasoned educators (who engage with parents about the well-being of their children) but by politicians, bureaucrats, think tanks, businesspeople, foundation functionaries, and pundits—few of whom have been in a school since they got their diploma—our nation's education system will be in deep trouble.[12]

Public librarianship suffers from the same "deep trouble." Like public education, public librarians—and the library and information science scholars who focus on them—have been slow to agree on measurements that define benefit or impact, especially for public libraries. Rather than utilizing statistical methodologies from other scholarly disciplines, public librarians have allowed their measurements to continue to be stated as an archaic industrial production model (inputs and outputs) or as sets of simplistic rankings (e.g., the HAPLER Index[13] and the Most Literate Cities Index).[14]

These ranking systems are so useless for measurements of impact—which is what the "resilient cities" term encompasses—that they are not even in the right domain. In an articulate *New Yorker* article critiquing college rankings, Malcolm Gladwell points out how *US News and World Report*'s college and university rankings are in reality attestations of the overall strength of the institution's reputation (i.e., its brand) rather than an objective measurement of its various statistical indicators of achievement. The article contains this quote from Robert Morris, who runs the *US News* college-ranking team:

> We're not saying that we're measuring educational outcomes. . . . We're not saying we're social scientists, or we're subjecting our rankings to some peer-review process. We're just saying we've made this judgment. We're saying we've interviewed a lot of experts, we've developed these academic indicators, and we think these measures measure quality schools.[15]

Summarizing his impressions of this comment, Gladwell writes,

> As answers go, that's up there with the parental "Because I said so." But Morse is simply being honest. If we don't understand what the right proxies for college quality are, let alone how to represent those proxies in a comprehensive, heterogeneous grading system, then our rankings are inherently arbitrary.[16]

The same thing can be said of the HAPLER Index and the Literate Cities rankings of public libraries. Both are illusory in creating estimates of library contributions to community resiliency. Their contribution to the library field is little more than the inflation of a few professional egos.

A legal issue

Readers of this chapter might be able to argue that this discussion of measures of impact or benefit was "merely academic," and therefore of little consequence, if funding agencies increasingly weren't looking for such measures as ratification of an agency's social benefit to validate their support.[17] The greatest legal push for accountability and quantifying outcomes for all libraries comes from a specific federal law. In 1993 the federal government passed the Government Performance and Results Act (GPRA).[18] Addressing its constituent libraries and museums, the Institute of Museum and Library Services summarizes the effect of the law this way:

> This law requires every government agency to establish specific performance goals for each of its programs, preferably with performance indicators stated in objective, quantifiable, and measurable terms. Agencies must report on their level of achievement in reaching these goals on an annual basis. The effects of GPRA are also trickling down to state and local government agencies that are using the lead of the federal government to require evidence that all public dollars are well spent.
>
> This is not just a government issue. A similar emphasis on accountability is being incorporated into funding guidelines for most major foundations. From all sides, museums and libraries are receiving a clear message: If they are to compete for both public and private funds in an accountability environment, they must develop evaluation practices that provide the most compelling picture of the impact of their services.[19]

The passage of GPRA thus forms a legal landmark in changing the way that school, university, and public libraries *must* measure their successful performance and their impact. Libraries that receive federal money *must* comply with the law and in the most objective terms set up and meet outcome and performance goals. At the same time, most libraries find that nonfederal granting and gifting agencies—and even wealthy, philanthropically inclined individuals—increasingly require the same kind of statistical measures in proposals, work statements, and project reports submitted to them.

With or without legislation similar to the federal GPRA, state and local governments, including school boards, library boards, and state university boards of regents now often request similar outcome and impact measurements. As well, foundations and even some individual givers who hold out the opportunity to provide significant donations want a close accounting of how their money is spent and the results it produces. Financial auditors and accountants, meanwhile, push for higher standards from the expenditure side of library operations. In the age of accountability, just like other government and institutional agencies, libraries are being told that if they want the money, they have to justify its good use and high impact.

Meanwhile, medicine and medical schools, which are hugely tied into public and private-sector funding sources, through the past decade have devised a means to measure every aspect of performance as part of various systems of "evidence-based management."[20] At some point in the not-too-distant future, especially if the U.S. economy remains in the doldrums for several more years, evidence-based management will catch on in libraries as it has in hospitals.[21]

If professional librarians are going to seriously deal with their positive impact on urban resiliency, their first effort needs to be to articulate exactly how their benefits can be measured.[22] It is no coincidence that three colleagues and I set out to apply economic cost-benefit analysis (CBA) to the services of individual libraries in 1993, at the time when Congress was considering the legislation that became GPRA. This methodology is not designed to establish another ranking system but to create a conservative, quantitative estimate of the benefits of the services that legal constituents receive from individual libraries or library systems. CBA is a long-tested and often-used methodology developed by academic economists.

Various library systems have enjoyed CBA estimates over the past half decade, but the St. Louis study remains the most comprehensively tested methodology, in that we used the same methodology to estimate the benefits of the services of fifteen different library systems. The unique aspect of our valuation of benefits studies was that some were high—upwards of $3 for every $1 invested—and some were low: three of the fifteen did not come close to returning a matching $1 in value for every $1 invested.

The conclusions of this study and the many other public library CBA studies which have been done in other cities with somewhat different methodologies show sufficient statistical variance to suggest that different libraries would vary greatly in their measurable contribution to urban resiliency, just as they vary in the value of the services they provide.[23]

To reiterate: without further study, attestations of library contribution to resilient communities are little more than faith-based assertions of belief, not evidence-based case studies leading to a more broadly applicable thesis about library contributions to the resiliency of communities.

Resiliency changes with the times

Along with methodology, there is the issue of change. As times change, the factors that make communities resilient may shift as well. Right now, the economic downturn is making most cities consider how to improve their economic situation.

Nothing so quickly elicits obfuscating sound bites from a city's elected officials than the erratic gales of recession. Good city administrators plan, make, and implement policy to avoid economic misfortune. They create "rainy-day funds" that will help them stave off economic crises. They search everywhere for "soft" money to add to their regular budget lines to help them stave off dramatic cuts to regular staff and services when regular budgets seem insufficient. The smartest of the officials are always conservative in their finances because they know that public revenues at some point will go down. And, like good scouts of every stripe, they want to "be prepared" to avoid financial crises.

And, just now, the monster that is eating up American federal, state, and local government (including almost all public libraries) is the Great Recession, which for the past year or so has always been capitalized to designate its significance as opposed to the Great Depression of the 1930s. Caught in the foggy miasma of local, state, regional, and national politics, elected officials continue to use the same kind of optimistic sound bites they have been using, but, all of us are told, there is no more money available.

In this richest of all nations, we are told that taxes cannot be raised to pay for essential services. Instead, we are informed that local government agencies—including public libraries—can deliver high-level services using low-paid clerks or volunteers where previously job tables called for skilled professionals or well-trained library technicians.

During upturns in the economy, elected officials often say to libraries, "Because you are so efficient, you can do lots more services with only a little bit more money." And, in the first stages of a severe downturn, libraries are told they can do at least as much as they are doing in times of affluence with somewhat less money. Then as it becomes clear that the Great Recession is hitting public revenues hard, libraries are told that they can do "at least as well" with far, far less revenue. Finally, libraries are told that the government will keep funding police, firefighters, and water and sewer departments because they are essential. But public subsidies for school lunches, medical care for the poor, medication for the poor who are mentally ill—and public libraries—"are not essential." So these can be cut drastically or even ended, becoming ghosts of their former service positions in their communities. Then when such services are not used because they are ghosts, political leaders who made the cuts cry, "See, we told you! These services were not essential. People can live without them."

A noteworthy example of this trend may be seen in Charlotte, North Carolina, bastion of the New South's formerly thriving growth economy which was based on the idea that low taxes, no unions, and government-assisted, private-sector growth is the only correct key to a bright future in twenty-first-century "free-market" economic heaven. When Charlotte's administrative staff looked around after assessing the Charlotte-Mecklenburg County government budget cuts for 2010, they realized that Charlotte's internationally recognized model-library system was one of the state's biggest losers, and slashed 30 percent from its $23 million budget.[24] Assessing the damage, Charles M. Brown, the Public Library of Charlotte and Mecklenburg's library director, made the necessary firings and layoffs, and then resigned. The cause was not hard to find: city fathers decided that a great deal of branch library services could be operated by volunteers and idiosyncratic donations from local governments.[25]

This example shows how national events can focus library operations onto just one issue: getting enough money to operate what library professionals would consider a minimally viable system. This kind of budget cutting treats public library services as peripheral rather than essential.

Are public libraries essential?

In these difficult times, then, how can public libraries make their case for contributing to their cities' resilience? What I hope I have established to this point in this chapter is that "urban resiliency" generally or of one city specifically requires thoughtful definition. If the national economy is worse than at any time in U.S. history except for the Great Depression of the 1930s, then nearly all public library contributions to urban resiliency probably need to involve mechanisms for helping heat up the local, regional, or national economy. Would this kind of basic jobs-building activity be seen as an essential service? By community influentials? By professional librarians?

There is a striking lack of discussion about essentiality in library literature. Who decides what is essential in American government services or in library services?

The most important qualification for essentiality—at least when it comes to the overall interests of the commonwealth—comes from the federal government. Waterways and highways are essential, and federal revenues and federal agency expertise is applied to them. When railroads carried the mail, they were essential, though there is lots of debate now over the essentiality of Amtrak and even more debate over urban transit. The U.S. mail used to be more essential than it is now, but the federal government regulates its profitability so that it has to mostly pay for itself while delivering junk mail at very low rates. Nutritional meals for school children are usually regarded as essential. Poor children not in school, however, are left to the vicissitudes of TANF (Temporary Assistance for Needy Families) and SNAP (Supplemental Nutrition Assistance Program). As can be seen in these examples, the determination of governmental conditions of essentiality is as much political as it is a matter of the national interest.

When Hurricane Katrina hit New Orleans, after examining a request for federal disaster-relief funds to help the Cameron Parish (LA) Public Library rebuild quickly after the disaster, FEMA (the Federal Emergency Management Agency) refused emergency funding, declaring that libraries were not essential services. Writing in *Public Library Quarterly*, the Louisiana state librarian, Rebecca Hamilton, responded to the negative FEMA designation by reporting the huge demand for library services after Katrina and Rita, and how the Louisiana State Library coordinated public library efforts to meet the needs of displaced residents.[26]

Better news about the federal definition of library essentiality came at the January 2011 Midwinter ALA Conference when ALA Washington Office executive director Emily Sheketoff announced that FEMA had, on January 7, decided to change its policy to permit public libraries to apply for temporary emergency relocation and support.[27]

The smallness of the benefit could be seen a month later when President Barack Obama proposed cutting funding for the IMLS (Institute of Museum and Library Services) from $282 million to $243 million and the size of the allocation for the LSTA (Library Services and Technology Act) went from $214 million to $193 million. The good news was that the cuts were relatively small, and the president at least sent the IMLS budget line to Congress with money on it. Previously both presidents George W. Bush and Bill Clinton had sent their annual executive draft budgets to Congress with zeros on these lines for libraries and museums, knowing that Congress would add in amounts. However, in the meantime, the national executives and their spokespersons could use the zero presidential budget lines to help make their overall proposals seem like they had submitted a balanced budget.

Thus, FEMA can now declare destroyed libraries as "essential" as of February 2011. However, it may take a lot more presidents before one of them does for libraries what President Dwight Eisenhower did for highways in 1954 when he declared that the nation absolutely had to have an interstate express highway system to move troops and machinery to defend the nation. At the moment he made that executive declaration, the federal funding spigot for highways turned on, and it has never been shut off since. Highways now are a matter of national interest. They are essential, and President Eisenhower and the Congress made them so. Until national, state, and local governments can be persuaded to declare the essential nature of public library work, stable funding will remain a paramount library problem.

Urban resiliency and library self-interest

Two well-known economic theories about how to increase employment in an economy driven by manufacturing, consumption, and services form the context of public-sector action during a major economic downturn like the Great Recession. One of these theories—that of John Maynard Keynes—involves direct public expenditure, including those made from government borrowing, to spend in ways that create a multiplier effect, so that consumers spend their wages generated in part by direct government spending. Milton Friedman and other Neo-classical economists, on the other hand—and going all the way back to Adam Smith—argue that the free market will find the best way: just hold down taxes, cut expenditures, and let individuals decide how to spend and invest their money. These expenditures by the many will accrue to society's best interests. In the Great Recession, there has been a resurgence in Keynes's popularity, but free-market advocates have strong voices as well and seem to be carrying the day.[28]

The idea that libraries contribute to urban resiliency has a foot in both theories, though one is more firmly based than the other. The most visible way that libraries can contribute to the local economy is through direct investment—that is, through building construction, purchase of services in the free market, and expenditures on salaries, especially those for well-paying jobs.

Construction

For the public, the most visible economic impact for public expenditure is through construction: in bad economic times, libraries help their economies by providing construction jobs.

My former employer, the St. Louis Public Library, is following this policy. In the midst of the Great Recession, it is using tax credits and a Triple A bond rating to obtain the funds to sustain a multimillion-dollar rehabilitation and modernization of the hundred-year-old Central Library. From a dollar standpoint, this library project currently is one of the largest public construction projects in the city of St. Louis. The library, therefore, is a major source of new construction jobs.

And the library is a major power in making the city of St. Louis and the St. Louis region more economically resilient.

Job-seeking

A second way to contribute to urban resiliency—specifically the ability to recover from a major economic downturn—is to help people find jobs. The Enoch Pratt Library in Baltimore offers a good example of this behavior. Over the last decade, Pratt has added hundreds of public-use computers, some of which are in a Jobs Center located in the Business and Technology Collections of the main library. Pratt has reassigned and trained staff members to help people learn computer skills, prepare resumes, fill out job applications, and write grant applications for their religious, social, and cultural organizations. Such activities are the foundation of grassroots economic development. They provide critical assistance in helping people train for, find, and get better jobs.[29]

Many other urban library systems have put job help units into the service areas of at least one of their libraries. These include but are hardly limited to the public libraries in Seattle, Denver, Los Angeles, Toronto, Baltimore, Milwaukee, Madison, and Charlotte, all which show up in the first thirty entries of a crude but effective Google search, "job help by public libraries." Libraries almost always have been active in helping users find jobs; since the beginning of the Great Recession, they have been more proactive and communicative about their effort.

English literacy

A third way that libraries contribute to urban resiliency involves literacy—early childhood literacy to help kids get ready to succeed in schools; primary literacy or teaching kids to read with imagination and meaning; adult literacy to overcome poor schooling or ESL (English as a Second Language) issues of being a foreign-language speaker in a country that has trouble tolerating any language except English in business, law, or the responsibilities of citizenship. Most libraries have focused on one or more aspects of literacy since their beginnings. At a time when so many schools seem to be underperforming, and there seems to be such malice against the immigrants who make such critical contributions to the U.S. economy, library emphasis on literacy deserves significant attention—and considerable resources.

E-government

A fourth activity that could help urban resiliency in the Great Recession is when a library serves as a highly functioning, locally focused e-government center. Paul Jaeger and John Carlo Bertot have provided a good overview of public library e-government functioning in a recent article that is heavily geared to federal information.[30] The government information that the local citizens of a library district frequently need is from local government, including local ordinances, licenses, and specifications and standards for contracting for publicly funded jobs. In all but the ordinance category, a library would do well to give special attention to how DBEs (Disadvantaged Business Enterprises), WBEs (Women-Owned Business Enterprises), and MBEs (Minority Business Enterprises) can go about meeting the specialized contracting requirements. One of the finest moments in my own St. Louis Public Library occurred when a local minority contractor returned to thank our reference staff for the help he had been given in winning a substantial subcontract for a New York City public works contract. Running a Foundation Grants Center is another powerful tool to demonstrate how a library helps build capital accumulation and expenditure.

Helping the poor

Finally, because illiteracy on the part of both adults and children is more prevalent among poorer populations than among those with higher incomes, libraries need to focus on their services to poor persons, including the homeless, the abused, and other dependent populations. No library services are more essential than those which librarians provide to those who have little. Such services can be like those listed in the previous paragraphs or they can scan local ordinances and other kinds of electronic information, provide homework help to latchkey children, and provide instruction in how to use computers to work effectively in a networked environment. Homework help for kids fits into this category. If the adult population has a high incidence of low or problem literacy and little experience with success in schools, libraries can and should help kids be successful in school through offering homework help. No activity is a better start to building a sense of the possibilities for lifelong learning than learning how to be successful at school and at work. Homework help is especially needed to aid kids caught in one of the frequent poverty problems of our time. To cite a bus-side advertisement from my city of residence: under the picture of a young man, the caption says, "This young man spent 45 minutes last night working on a class term paper. And he spent nine hours at a job earning enough money to stay in school."[31]

Library services like the ones described above are time- and place-specific. They provide direct assistance to large numbers of urban citizens, helping advance the community's economy in ways that can be measured.[32]

American public libraries fulfill their commonweal-service function when they provide visible essential services like those summarized in the earlier paragraphs in this section. Why these functions? Because they are visible, measurable, and useful to large numbers of needy community residents. It would be easy to find or develop a methodology to calculate the benefit of any of the library user services discussed previously in this section.

They are also politically popular. Most citizens are glad to know that libraries are helping children and people who have less rather than more resources. These citizens tend to be supportive of such activities, especially if the library's communications program has pointed this out over and over, through occasionally bringing in new timely service responses and the appropriate carrying forward of sustained services. Nothing pleases voters more than to believe that they are getting their money's worth from their libraries, either because of the services they use or because of the services that they believe are valuable to the community even though they do not use them.

What about other kinds of library activities? The answer to this question needs to start with what your library's users want and need. Now, a "hard question" regarding essentiality: what if a library's users seem to only need or want books, particularly fiction books? NoveList and NextReads founder Duncan Smith points out, "Books are the Library's Brand."[33] Where does fiction fit into the reality of essential services? Does fiction have an important impact on the building of community resiliency?

Next, add one other reality about public library use: how should we regard a study that shows that over 50 percent of a library's circulation output is the checkout of electronic materials—that is, CDs, DVDs, and electric downloads—obtained through the library and one of its vendors that sell electronic rights to libraries? Figures like this have popped up increasingly in the last few years.

Unfortunately, discussion over both the libraries branded by their books and the libraries which appear to serve mostly as free or very cheap electronic or video stores have generated few rational discussions. Hardly anyone in library circles has asked, "What are good sources of creative ideas?" Or, "what turns on imagination?" Instead, discussions examining the value of broad reading as an economic growth activity or how serendipity actually works have been overshadowed by ideological rants that have mirrored concerns like "should we allow the poor to have cheap or free fun?" That, of course, has origins that can be tracked to the "bread and circuses" debates in ancient Rome.

There are two realities reflected here. The first is that both books and electronic story and game utilization are increasingly subjected to issues involving out-of-pocket costs and convenience (i.e., the use of time). Circulation of books and journals from academic libraries is falling. Overall the rate is about 2.5 percent per year. Newspaper circulation is declining, with portable electronic devices picking up the daily or weekly paper's news reporting and cultural analysis and publicity function. Meanwhile, online buying and selling has decimated local want ad and personal ad revenue.

Individuals, families, and businesses are making decisions about what they will spend and how much time they will utilize to get not only paper-based newspapers but also books and electronic stories, documentaries, or games from the library. Some people are always going to want cheap or free—and convenient—entertainment, especially for their children. Of course, high checkout rates demonstrate the demand for electronic entertainment and cultural products. However, we already can see the new trends that are affecting electronic entertainment. The first is downloading media from the Net from such services as Hulu, Amazon, Netflix, and AOL, to name only four prominent players in the field.[34] The second is that publishers seek to gain all possible value from copyrights.

The great advantage of the networked information and entertainment cloud is that nothing ever has to die. The great disadvantage of the Net cloud is that hardly anything that once had value as a "publication," whether on paper, discretely electronic, or produced and held in the cloud, will ever lose sufficient value that it will ever be fully free. If you consider this idea an exaggeration, take a look at least in the United States, where there will always be some business that will attempt to crank the latest pennies out of the most recent showing of any production ever offered.[35] Public libraries experienced the first wave of this reality recently when one publisher informed them that items which had unlimited plays initially now had a limitation on the number of plays. The net impact for libraries is that libraries might have to buy 25 electronic copies of a James Patterson novel, and as soon as any one of those copies had been checked out 10 times, the library would have to buy another level of copyright access, if you will—another copy, to keep users happy.[36]

Whether or not your library's leaders decide that books or electronic-formatted audio and video products are essential and even deserve a place in your resilient community assemblage of programs I leave up to you. My only advice for this category of library material is that library managers should not get so caught up in serving the needs of those right now that they don't watch for the startling dramatic changes that keep sweeping through the national and international marketplace. In Japan, for example, where housing units are small even by new couple standards of the United States, more than sixty companies have quickly appeared to scan individuals' book collections so that they can be removed from living or work quarters. Here is a latent demand for living space that already is quickly reducing the number of book volumes held by individuals and families as part of their space adaptation.[37]

Rules for library contributions to urban resiliency

In this chapter I have attempted to frame some of the major issues around the idea that public libraries contribute to a community's resiliency. I have no doubt that other scholars and practitioners will decide that I have either overemphasized or neglected other issues. Such criticisms will be useful because they suggest how little any of us really know about how to shape all the factors that need to be considered when making sense out of the very complex problem of how educational institutions like public libraries can have a measurable impact on community resiliency. Our problem quite simply is that there is no body of literature sufficiently large to draw a complete picture of what libraries ought to include in the program and service set that contributes to resilient communities.

Here is my most recent list of rules for how libraries can best position themselves to contribute to community resiliency in the era of the Great Recession:

1. Don't assume that the circulation of books or even electronic programs (DVDs, CDs, and their legatees) are a foundation on which libraries can build a bright future for longer than perhaps another decade. The shocks of discontinuity are going to provide as many if not more avenues to the future than continuities.

2. Don't assume that serving as a community center or a community education center is a discrete function performed only by public libraries. Many other institutions and people—including teachers, schools, colleges, universities, churches, parents, and good friends—contribute to community education, some in more demonstrably direct ways than do public libraries. When a kid learns to read by third grade, should the public library take credit? Why ask? As a recorded fact, I and hundreds of thousands and probably millions of other kids could read before we went to a library or to school for the first time.

Sure, lots and lots of famous people say they were inspired to read or to take some action because of something that happened at a public library. Good! But what about the millions of others who did not have such an experience?

3. Analyze the library's community. What is the demographic character of a public library's target population? Some libraries—like Detroit or St. Louis—have a high level of poverty and a high level of minority ethnic or racial population. King County and Pierce County in suburban Seattle tend to operate at the other end of the socioeconomic scale. These populations do not have the same needs. One population needs more adult basic literacy help than another. Another needs more access to English as a second language than another. Some library districts have reasonably good schools, where libraries can serve their traditional supplementary homework-help function. Others have schools so bad that school libraries or media centers are little more than a joke, a fact revealed when entire urban systems of public schools are de-certified as degree-granting institutions—which is exactly what has happened in St. Louis. To sum up, library target population needs vary—sometimes by a little and sometimes hugely.\

4. Don't expect conversations with users to produce too much information about their future needs. Ask users and prospective users which current or new library services are essential in their personal and community lives just now. However, most library users, just like most library employees, have enormous trouble thinking beyond the here and now to consider the services they use or want.

5. Libraries should think through, authorize, and publicize a proactive mission for themselves, to improve the individual, family, and community life of all citizens, including current nonusers.

6. Measure the impact or benefits of your library's services on individuals and on specific groups like businesses, teachers, and nonprofit organizations. Don't depend on the measurements of others, especially those who construct "institutional rankings." The principal reason you do measurements of your services is to help your administration make evidence-based library management decisions designed to achieve certain well-articulated goals. There is an old but still relevant cliché in business economics: "If you can't measure it, you can't manage it." Contrast that with a sentiment not uncommon among library professionals, to the effect that "statistical measurement of library benefits is insane because so much of what we as librarians do cannot be measured." Essentially: "Do what I say, because that's what I believe."

7. In this critical time in which computer-based electronic recording and communications is dramatically shifting the cultural, economic, and social organization of our society, libraries need to recognize that cell phones and handheld computers are replacing paper, credit cards, and library cards. Libraries must

overcome their institutional resistance to participation in the latest forms of electronic identification, communication, and business transaction. The director of the Roanoke (TX) Public Library made the point well in an early 2011 issue of *American Libraries* when he wrote,

> The library world . . . has done a poor job of keeping up with new technologies over the past decade. . . . The world of information exchange is in constant flux, and we are slow to change. Our risk-averse conservative approach has made many of us maladaptive. . . . Over the past year, you may have seen store clerks scanning customers' mobile phones. Some are using coupons sent to their phones by the store, but others are simply using their phones in place of reward cards.[38]

8. Reach out to make partnerships of all kinds that will increase your impact on community resiliency. Public libraries are a very small business, much smaller than the public school, law enforcement, professional baseball or football or other major sports teams, welfare organizations, or, in some cases, even the totality of homeless services—the list goes on and on. Libraries need agents, telling their stories, and libraries need allies—not just users who like them and will stand beside them and defend them when their funding is attacked—as it surely will be—unless your library district is some well-guarded piece of public service heaven.

9. Public libraries began as adjuncts to public schools. Their primary legal responsibility is education. The library educational role can be broadly or narrowly defined, but defined it must be, including defining the limits of educational services. Above all else, libraries must be educational if they are going to be true to the corporate charters and other state and local legislation that created most of them.

10. Libraries need to consider how they are contributing to the sustainability of their communities. And they should work very hard to make sure they are contributing to that sustainability—in specific and measurable ways.

11. Libraries need to communicate their contribution to their communities at the neighborhood, individual, and family level—in multiple ways and in multiple times. That includes pointing out what the community will lose if this institution is not present and if it does not provide certain services. That communication needs to address issues of user and community self-interest—and, yes, these two interests may contradict.

12. As part of positively impacting the sustainability of your community, your institution ought to find several different sources of funding including grants, donations, and earmarked government funds.

13. If you follow these admonitions, your library will be political, which all libraries must be most of the time. Most attacks on libraries for whatever reason are political. High-minded statements of principle generated in Chicago or Washington, DC, are not going to do the job when what is needed is a face-to-face meeting between a large donor who will speak on behalf of the library to an elected official or a foundation executive.

14. The last rule is the hardest. Within your institutional vision, create some new rules or rules better than the ones here for improving your library's institutional impact on your community's resiliency. *Library contributions to community resiliency are not automatic but intentional, not necessarily dramatic but always sustained, and not part of a rankings game but demonstrably measurable and defendable with your publics.* Remember that definition, measurement, and communication with residents about library impact are an ongoing part of doing library business. With this information infrastructure, a public library's commitment to urban resiliency is not just public relations or marketing but a matter of building and maintaining a relationship with an institution's host constituency—that is, its community and its residents—to keep pointing out how the library is working to improve individual lives and the community's resiliency.

NOTES

1. "St. Louis," *Wikipedia,* http://en.wikipedia.org/wiki/St._Louis _Missouri#Demographics.

2. "New Orleans Diaspori," *Wikipedia,* http://en.wikipedia.org/wiki/New_Orleans _diaspora.

3. "Abiline Kansas," *City-Data.com,* www.city-data.com/city/Abilene-Kansas.html.

4. Rebecca Hamilton, "The State Library of Louisiana and Public Libraries' Response to Hurricanes: Issues, Strategies and Lessons," *Public Library Quarterly* 30, no. 1 (2011), 40–53.

5. The Abilene Public Library's Facebook page on February 28, 2011, was at www .facebook.com/pages/Abilene-Public-Library/225814280638. Some of the facts in this paragraph were ascertained in an interview with the APL's library director in late February 2011.

6. Leslie Edmonds Holt and Glen E. Holt, *Public Library Services for the Poor: Doing All We Can* (Chicago: American Library Association, 2010).

7. "St Louis Public Library," *Wikilou,* www.wikilou.com/lou/index.php?title= St._Louis_Public_Library.

8. Author's personal archives.

9. Jason Pontin, "Awaiting the Day When Everyone Writes Software," *New York Times Online,* January 28, 2007, www.nytimes.com/2007/01/28/business/ yourmoney/28slip.html?_r=1&th&emc=th&oref=slogin.

10. Ibid.

11. Robert H. Bremner, *From the Depths: The Discovery of Poverty in the United States* (New York: New York University Press, 1956). Chapter 9 points out this investigative orientation.

12. Diane Ravich, "The Death of Federalism," *Education Week,* January 25, 2011, http://blogs.edweek.org/edweek/Bridging-Differences/accountability/. This is a recent posting on accountability in a published dialogue that has been going on for years.

13. Ray Lyons, "Unsettling Scores: An Evaluation of Hennen's American Public Library Ratings," *Public Library Quarterly* 26, nos. 1–2 (2007).

14. Glen E. Holt, "We're Number One! We're Number One! We're Number One!" *Library Leadership Network Commons,* March 9, 2006. Author's personal copy; content no longer available online.

15. Malcolm Gladwell, "The Order of Things: What College Rankings Really Tell Us," *New Yorker,* February 14, 2011, 68–75.

16. Ibid.

17. Leslie Edmonds Holt, Glen E. Holt, and Stratton Lloyd, *Library Success: A Celebration of Library Innovation, Adaptation and Problem Solving* (Boston: EBSCO, 2006).

18. GPRA has its own website at www.whitehouse.gov/omb/mgmt-gpra/gplaw2m .html. Most every aspect of the law is clearly analyzed on this site. A search of the full name of GPRA will bring up myriad websites that analyze the law's terms.

19. Beverly Sheppard, introduction to "Perspectives on Outcome-Based Evaluation for Museums and Libraries," www.imls.gov/pdf/pubobe.pdf.

20. A recent textbook on this subject is Janet Houser and Kathleen S. Oman, *Evidence-Based Practice: An Implementation Guide for Healthcare Organizations* (Sudbury, MA; Jones and Bartlett Learning, 2010).

21. The single best overview of library measurement is Joseph R. Matthews, *Measuring for Results: The Dimension of Public Library Effectiveness* (Westport, CT: Libraries Unlimited, 2003).

22. Donald Elliott, Glen E. Holt, Sterling Hayden, and Leslie Edmonds Holt, *Measuring Your Library's Value: How to Do a Cost-Benefit Analysis for Your Public Library* (Chicago: American Library Association, 2006).

23. Americans for Libraries Council, "Worth Their Weight: An Assessment of the Evolving Field of Library Valuation," www.ila.org/advocacy/pdf/ WorthTheirWeight.pdf.

24. Michael Kelly, "LJ's 2010 Budget Survey: Bottoming Out?" *LibraryJournal.com,* January 15, 2011, www.libraryjournal.com/lj/ communitymanaginglibraries/888434-273/ljs_2010_budget_survey_bottoming .html.csp.

25. Mark Price, "Charlotte Mecklenburg Library Director Resigns," *WCNC.com,* January 19, 2011, 3www.wcnc.com/news/local/Library-director-Charles-Brown -resigns-114220814.html.

26. Rebecca Hamilton, "The State Library of Louisiana and Public Libraries' Response to Hurricanes: Issues, Strategies and Lessons," *Public Library Quarterly* 30 no. 1 (2011): 40–53.

27. Kelly, "LJ's 2010 Budget Survey: Bottoming Out?"

28. "John Maynard Keynes," *Wikipedia,* http://en.wikipedia.org/wiki/John_Maynard _Keynes. This summary is convenient, at about the right level of sophistication for this chapter, and has notes for other more advanced sources. For Neoclassical economics, see the *Wikipedia* reference with that title.

29. For more on the Enoch Pratt Library, see chapter 4 by Vanessa Francis in this volume.

30. Paul T. Jaeger, and John Carlo Bertot, "Responsibility Rolls Down: Public Libraries and the Social and Policy Obligations of Ensuring Access to E-Government and Government Information," *Public Library Quarterly* 30, no. 2 (2011): 91–116.

31. Holt and Holt, *Public Library Services for the Poor.*

32. Elliott, Holt, Hayden, and Holt in *Measuring Your Library's Value* outline this methodology and how individual libraries can manage the process.

33. Duncan Smith, "Books: An Essential Part of Essential Libraries," *Public Library Quarterly* 30, no. 4 (2011): 257–69.

34. Annoyed Librarian, "Library Videos Won't Survive, and There Go Our Circ Stats," *LibraryJournal,* September 22, 2010, http://blog.libraryjournal.com/ annoyedlibrarian/2010/09/22/videos-circ-stats/.

35. For a very nice recent summary, see Brad Templeton, "10 Big Myths about Copyright Explained," www.templetons.com/brad/copymyths.html.

36. Josh Hadro, "HarperCollins Puts 26-Loan Cap on EBook Circulations," *LibraryJournal.com,* February 25, 2011, www.libraryjournal.com/lj/home/889452 -264/harpercollins_caps_loans_on_ebook.html.csp.

37. Pavel Alpeyev and Yoshinori Eki, "Book Business Stacks Up for Scanners in Japan," *Seattle Times,* March 2, 2011, A11, A12.

38. Jesse Ephraim, "Why Must a Card Be a Card?" *American Libraries,* January/ February, 2011, 31.

Jennifer Hoyer

Finding room for everyone
Libraries confront social exclusion

A local homeless man once told me he was grateful that the library allows patrons to drink coffee, although food is still banned inside the building. The library, he explained, is the only place he can stay warm during the day, but that he'd be kicked out if he falls asleep. Frequent coffee refills allow him to remain inside his only refuge from cold Canadian winters.

Every library has its own policy on allowing coffee through the doors, and every library has its own approach to serving homeless, vulnerable, or marginalized members of the community. Decisions about providing library services to marginalized groups boil down to institutional beliefs about the role of libraries in dealing with social exclusion, a mission which is not universally accepted.[1]

Briefly defined, social exclusion encompasses the social aspects of poverty: not only poverty with regard to material goods and resources, but also the inability to participate in social activities, a lack of access to services, and educational and cultural poverty.[2] Persons or groups may be marginalized and excluded based on ethnic origin, gender, sexuality, physical or mental disability, education, employment, and economic status.[3] Aside from reducing the quality of life of marginalized persons, social exclusion threatens social cohesion within communities and limits opportunities for widespread economic prosperity.[4] Social exclusion therefore threatens the health of communities and must be taken seriously by society as a whole.

A high level of adaptability is necessary on the part of institutions to meet the needs of socially excluded groups, as they are often socially excluded because their needs have not been anticipated. Adaptability is one of the core tenets of resilience.[5] As Chris McLaughlin explains, resilience means "finding new ways (and maybe renewing old ways) of coping with an unpredictable future."[6]

If communities are to become more resilient, then they must find ways to adapt to the needs of socially excluded populations, by setting up measures that can proactively prepare for the needs of marginalized groups as well as prevent exclusion in the first place. Communities that are working to combat exclusion have greater potential for success if they enlist the support of public libraries, which are in many ways ideally situated to welcome marginalized populations and provide programs and services that combat social exclusion. This chapter explains how this adaptability in response to social problems fits with the mandate of public libraries; examines why and how libraries should confront social exclusion; and looks at the Atwater Library and Computer Centre (ALCC) in Westmount, Québec, as an illustration of how this has been successfully accomplished.

Libraries adapting to change

Every community faces unique challenges with regard to social exclusion, based on the community's demographic and economic profile. To remain healthy and resilient, a community must be flexible and adaptive to constantly changing demographics and emerging needs. However, many institutions are incapable of adapting their programs and services quickly enough to deal proactively with potential issues relating to exclusion. Community institutions often have mandates, matched by budget designations, which focus programs and services on specific needs or community groups. For example, an after-school care center will only serve the needs of children in the community, and a Junior Chamber of Commerce provides resources for young professionals.

By contrast, public libraries have this adaptability built into their identity. The mandate of a library is to serve its user community. While special libraries may have a designated user group, the scope of a public library's mandate is traditionally geographic rather than demographic. Thus, as demographics within this geographic area change, the library's mandate would require that programs and services evolve to serve the changing community, and successful libraries constantly adapt their programming to serve their user community as needs arise. Recognizing that socially excluded groups exist within the library's geographic user community allows for proactive development of appropriate programs and services.

Social exclusion and libraries

While many national library associations have policies on social exclusion, and the International Federation of Library Associations initiated discussion on social exclusion at its 2007 World Congress, tension still exists over whether libraries should be responsible for dealing with socially excluded populations.[7] The

Department for Culture, Media and Sport in the United Kingdom set a precedent for welcoming marginalized groups into libraries with the publication of *Libraries for All: Social Inclusion in Public Libraries* in 1999, but opponents continue to voice their opinions.[8] Information science professor Blaise Cronin, for example, has described homeless people in the library as a "disruptive minority." Cronin is adamant that there is no room in libraries for antisocial conduct or, in essence, "different" behavior, and laments the fact that some libraries have been forced to ban patrons from bringing in bulky bags, stating that the situation should never have eroded this far.[9] Darrin Hodgetts and others describe a public library that brought in permanent security guards after complaints by staff and the public;[10] this action has been taken by many libraries. Libraries worry that the majority of their patrons will feel uncomfortable or unsafe if some marginalized and minority groups are encouraged to use the library. The issue is controversial and has been avoided by many library policy makers for fear of confrontation and disagreement.

Strong arguments have also been voiced in favor of library outreach to socially excluded groups. Annette DeFaveri, a children and youth librarian for the Vancouver Public Library, states that inclusiveness is part of a library's core values and not an optional add-on.[11] Indeed, Florida Atlantic University Librarian Rachael Cathcart notes that "the issues associated with users struggling with homelessness and mental illness have more or less become part of the fabric of public libraries."[12] Matthew Williamson, an education advisor with the University of London, points out that individuals or groups are socially excluded because they do not have access to resources that the rest of the population possess, and that the "the cessation of this injustice is a prime role of the public library."[13]

Library strategies for tackling social exclusion

When it comes to the nuts and bolts of reaching socially excluded groups through the library, employing a variety of options can account for the reality that no community deals with the same exclusion issues. In any situation, however, use of public libraries by the socially excluded is primarily for recreational purposes.[14] DeFaveri suggests greater use of library space for nonlibrary community programming, as well as removing financial barriers to access: rethinking policies on fines and membership costs for low-income individuals, and making memberships available to people without fixed addresses.[15]

Human resources are an integral part of a library's interaction with socially excluded groups. Culturally diverse staff can open doors to interaction with equally diverse users.[16] Staff must also learn to be sensitive to the unique needs of marginalized and vulnerable library users. Libraries can reach out to excluded groups by partnering with individuals and agencies in the community who have experience with these specific populations. Consultation and partnership with community associations, service agencies, and other local groups will inject new expertise which libraries can combine with their own resources and facilities to provide services that cannot or would not be offered elsewhere.[17]

In today's information society, information accessibility plays a key role in allowing all people to take part in community. As information providers, libraries and librarians find themselves in a position that no other organization can fill. They are able to help socially excluded individuals and groups overcome the disadvantages they otherwise face when accessing and using information.[18] Libraries can provide education opportunities for all ages and offer computer training. Many libraries provide language training and citizenship courses, or skills development and career preparation. The information required for all these tasks lies within a library's walls; by helping disadvantaged individuals access this information, libraries take a key role in helping everyone become active members of society and in creating more healthy, equitable communities.

The Atwater Library and Computer Centre: a legacy of meeting community needs

The Atwater Library and Computer Centre, located in Westmount, Québec (a separate municipality within the geographic boundaries of the city of Montréal), was founded in 1828 as the Mechanics' Institute of Montréal. The Mechanics' Institute movement, originating in Scotland in the early nineteenth century, promoted educational opportunities for tradesmen and their children. Mechanics' Institutes around the world provided some of the first adult education to social groups who did not have access to these opportunities elsewhere. As most Mechanics' Institutes evolved into publicly funded community libraries, often joining existing library systems, they brought their emphasis on education for the masses to the public library movement. Coming from this context, the ALCC draws on a 180-year legacy of working with disadvantaged social groups.

The ALCC facilities and resources are open to the public; while borrowing privileges require membership, there are no restrictions on information access, library use by nonmembers, or the length of time spent in the library. Unlike other Mechanics' Institutes, the ALCC did not become a publicly funded library. Instead it remains privately funded by membership fees, private donations, and a variety of community grants and other funding programs. This funding situation poses challenges, but it has also opened new doors for meeting the needs of marginalized groups in the community. The ALCC is able to make decisions regarding collection development and programming independent of the red tape that hampers proactive programming in some public institutions, allowing library services to be as flexible as necessary to meet the needs of the user community. Some of these programs and services are described below, as well as the community partnerships that have made them successful.

Situated on the border of the city of Westmount and the city of Montréal, the ALCC is in close proximity to a number of minority populations and vulnerable groups. The population of the city of Westmount is almost 30 percent immigrants; roughly 20 percent arrived in the five years preceding Canada's 2006 census.[19] The ALCC neighbors a YMCA temporary housing facility for refugee claimants. It is across the street from a children's hospital that draws patients from rural and impoverished communities around the province; some of these families face similar cultural and language barriers in the "big city" as the nearby refugee claimants. There are a large number of homeless persons in the area as well. The ALCC is one of the closest community libraries to the downtown Montréal area, making it a popular drop-in for homeless people during harsh weather. The ALCC is also situated in an area with an aging population. According to 2006 census data, 21 percent of the population in Westmount was over sixty-five.[20] In summary, the library is positioned in close proximity to several vulnerable or marginalized groups: immigrants, refugees, newcomers, homeless persons, and seniors.

Immigrants, refugees and newcomers

Immigrants, refugees, and newcomers are often excluded simply because they face language barriers and may have no permanent address, making it impossible to apply for a library card. Immigrants use the library for cost-effective leisure and entertainment, but the library can also help meet basic needs, such as online resources concerning housing, employment, or completing government paperwork related to immigrant or refugee status. Immigrants may also be interested in educational opportunities to help them find employment.[21] Appropriate library services for immigrants are best determined by identifying the needs of the population that an individual library will be serving.[22]

To determine local needs and reach this segment of the population, the ALCC has worked with neighborhood organizations to identify outreach opportunities. As mentioned above, libraries can help excluded groups by providing membership options that waive fees or do not require a fixed address. Since the neighboring YMCA opened its refugee center in 2001 the library has offered free computer center memberships to residential refugee claimants, giving them member pricing on computer use. A discounted full membership is available once these members acquire permanent housing.

The influx of refugees and other newcomers has highlighted language and cultural barriers. The ALCC draws on a cohort of 130 volunteers who speak a total of fifteen languages. Some of these volunteers first used the ALCC's services as refugee claimants, and they have returned to volunteer their time and language skills. As previously noted, culturally diverse staff can open library doors to ethnic groups within the community. To break down language barriers further, the ALCC has pursued partnerships to provide multilingual resources. Funding from the city of Westmount allowed for the creation of a multilingual collection of information resources for orienting oneself in the community.

Many new immigrants in this community are seeking to improve their English or learn other skills that will help them find employment. The ALCC's "Lifelong Learning Collection," developed in cooperation with other community service organizations, makes early literacy materials available to adults learning to read or learning English for the first time. A large collection of computer books and periodicals helps library users become familiar with computers or update their skills in various computer specializations.

The close relationship with the YMCA refugee center has highlighted a unique information need of new Canadians: they must complete specific online documents to apply for refugee status or residency. Another partnership with the neighboring municipality of the borough of Ville-Marie provided funding for new computers and communication hardware (webcams and microphones). This provides refugees and immigrants with access to the online information they need, and it also allows them to easily keep in touch with family back home.

Homelessness

Service to homeless populations sparks debate, as noted above, but many libraries including the ALCC are embracing these patrons. In a study to inform their own library services to the homeless, the staff at the San José Public Library reflected on what services the homeless population requires. They concluded that the information needs of homeless individuals will vary according to their circumstances, although a heavy emphasis can be placed on resources for meeting basic needs and help learning new skills for employability. Library programs and literacy resources are important, and the library should make programs and services available to homeless users who cannot obtain a library card because they do not have a permanent address.[23]

The ALCC has been welcoming to the significant population of people who are homeless in the area. There are no library programs unique to homeless users, but many existing programs and services are highly relevant. Computer center services are available without library membership—an important issue for patrons without permanent addresses. Literacy tools and other self-education resources are available for library patrons to use on-site without membership, and these are a great help to homeless patrons who want to find employment. Daily newspapers are also popular for their "help wanted" sections. As with all library patrons, homeless users are expected to be quiet and courteous to others. The official policy is that all members of the public can use the library as long as they do not disturb other patrons. Rules for library behavior are applied regardless of economic status. Thus, while policies on library use are firm, library use itself is flexible.

A core group of homeless patrons have learned that they are welcome and treated with respect in the building. They spend cold days at the reading desks, enjoying reference materials and periodicals. Others take advantage of "by-donation" coffee to warm up and stay alert. They are welcome to bring their bags in with them as long as they are not oversized or unpleasant in any way; again, this is a general rule that would apply to any library user, emphasizing equality of all patrons.

Seniors

The aging population presents a different set of issues. Many seniors are disconnected from the community because they suffer from accessibility and autonomy issues. The *Canadian Guidelines on Library and Information Services for Older Adults* explain that seniors have a wide range of needs. Libraries that wish to promote their services to seniors should ensure that they are reflecting the needs of seniors in their immediate community through collections, programs, and services. Library facilities should be safe and accessible, and librarians should treat older patrons with respect. Library programs can address technical skills, reading topics, and unique interests related specifically to seniors.[24] Many public libraries have focused on providing delivery of materials for homebound individuals, purchasing collection items in large print or on tape for seniors with sight impairments, and coordinating computer programs or reading groups that focus on issues pertinent to seniors. Libraries can also provide opportunities for seniors to volunteer in their community.[25]

Recognizing the mobility issues of several seniors in the neighborhood, the ALCC started a delivery service in 2010 to homebound residents with funding from Canadian Heritage and the borough of Ville-Marie. Telephone and online renewal have been promoted to seniors and are popular during winter months when icy roads make it difficult for older adults to get to the library to return their books.

Library collections and programs are developed with local seniors in mind. A sizable local Scottish community has helped fund the acquisition of books by Scottish authors or about Scotland. Best-selling fiction is also popular among older library users. Basic computer courses for word processing, e-mail applications, social media, and a variety of other computer programs fill up quickly. Special classes have taught participants how to use eBay, research genealogy, or make travel arrangements online. These allow seniors to communicate with distant family and to maintain a degree of independence.

Many of the ALCC's 130 volunteers are seniors. Volunteering gives them an opportunity to get out on a regular basis, to be involved in social activities, and to interact with like-minded individuals. Regular social events for volunteers build community for older adults in the area.

These programs and policies provide vulnerable groups in this neighborhood—immigrants, refugees, newcomers, people who are homeless, and seniors—with a place where they can know that their unique needs are acknowledged and respected. New programs are initiated on an ongoing, as-needed basis, in response to emerging demographic trends. As a result, minority and vulnerable populations have not been excluded but are instead embraced by an established community institution.

Communities tackle social exclusion together: strength in partnerships

It should be noted that the ALCC is not offering these services on its own. While the ALCC does not receive public funding, specific programs are funded by grants from local and national governments (as described above). Libraries can have greater impact if they involve other individuals and groups in partnerships for service provision.

These relationships are mutually beneficial. They allow local municipalities to participate in providing services that create inclusion and build for resilience. The city of Westmount and the neighboring borough of Ville-Marie are composed of dynamic and multifaceted populations. While the municipalities provide many core services for their residents, they are incapable of catering to every group: infrastructure, human resources, and bureaucracy are not flexible enough to offer a range of programs for every population segment. The ALCC, on the other hand, has space that can be adapted to meet the needs of the community. As a library, it also has a mandate to serve all members of the public. The partnership between funding partners and the ALCC creates an inclusive environment that none of these organizations would have the resources to provide in isolation.

Stronger libraries, stronger communities

Communities that recognize the great potential libraries offer and build on these strengths will discover new ways to combat exclusion, strengthen citizen engagement, and build brighter futures. Libraries that reach out to socially excluded members of their community are stronger for it, as they embrace a greater part of their mandate to provide information access. As a result of directed programming, adjusted membership policies, culturally sensitive and multilingual staffing, and enhanced access to relevant information, every demographic group can find a place for itself within the library. The ability of libraries to proactively adapt programs and services means that, in a community with an aware and involved library, no one needs to slip through the cracks.

NOTES

1. Sanford Berman, "Classism in the Stacks: Libraries and Poverty," *Journal of Information Ethics* (Spring 2007): 103–10.

2. Dave Muddiman, "Theories of Social Exclusion and the Public Library," in *Open to All?: The Public Library and Social Exclusion* (London: Council for Museums, Archives and Libraries, 2001), 1–15.

3. Briony Train, Pete Dalton, and Judith Elkin, "Embracing Inclusion: The Critical Role of the Library," *Library Management* 21, no. 9 (2000): 483.

4. Peter Donnelly and Jay Coakley, *The Role of Recreation in Promoting Social Inclusion* (Toronto: Laidlaw Foundation, 2002), vii, www.offordcentre.com/ VoicesWebsite/library/reports/documents/laidlaw/donnelly.pdf.

5. "5 Key Concepts of Resilience," adapted from Brian Walker and David Salt, "Resilience Thinking" (2006) in *Alternatives Journal* 36, no. 2 (2010): 19.

6. Chris McLaughlin, "Resilience 101," *Alternatives Journal* 36, no. 2 (2010): 18.

7. John Gehner, "Libraries, Low-Income People, and Social Exclusion," *Public Library Quarterly* 29 (2010): 39–40.

8. Darrin Hodgetts and others, "A Trip to the Library: Homelessness and Social Inclusion," *Social and Cultural Geography* 9 (2008): 933–53.

9. Blaise Cronin, "Library Journal: Commentary: The Dean's List: 'What a Library Is Not,'" *Indiana University Bloomington School of Library and Information Science*, www.slis.indiana.edu/news/story.php?story_id=497.

10. Hodgetts and others, "A Trip to the Library."

11. Annette DeFaveri, "Breaking Barriers: Libraries and Socially Excluded Communities," *Information for Social Change* 21 (Summer 2005): 27–34.

12. Rachael Cathcart, "Librarian or Social Worker: Time to Look at the Blurring Line?" *Reference Librarian* 49, no. 1 (2008): 90.

13. Matthew Williamson, "Social Exclusion and the Public Library: A Habermasian Insight," *Journal of Librarianship and Information Science* 32, no. 4 (December 2000): 180.

14. Ibid., 184.

15. DeFaveri, "Breaking Barriers."

16. Briony Birdi, Kerry Wilson, and Joanne Cocker, "The Public Library, Exclusion and Empathy: A Literature Review," *Library Review* 57, no. 8 (2008): 576–92.

17. Muddiman, "Theories of Social Exclusion."

18. Ibid.

19. Statistics Canada, "2006 Community Profile, Westmount, Québec," *Statcan.ca,* http://www12.statcan.ca.

20. Ibid.

21. Sondra Cuban, *Serving New Immigrant Communities in the Library* (Westport CT: Libraries Unlimited, 2007).

22. Ibid., 31.

23. Lydia N. Collins, Francis Howard, and Angie Miraflor, "Addressing the Needs of the Homeless: A San José Library Partnership Approach," *Reference Librarian* 50, no. 1 (2009): 112–13.

24. Canadian Library Association, Library Services to Older People Interest Group, "Canadian Guidelines on Library and Information Services for Older Adults" (2002), www.cla.ca/AM/Template.cfm?Section=Position_Statements&Template=/CM/ContentDisplay.cfm&ContentID=3029.

25. Pannaga Prasad, "Reference Services to Senior Groups in the San Antonio Public Library," *Reference Librarian* 50, no. 1 (2009): 102–6.

chapter four

Vanessa N. Francis

Baltimore's equalizer
Lessons in social equity from the Enoch Pratt Free Library

For all rich or poor, without distinction of race or color . . .
—Enoch Pratt, 1882

The above quote speaks to the belief of the Enoch Pratt Free Library's founder that books, and the acquisition of knowledge, should be available to citizens from every stratum of society. Since opening in 1886, the Pratt Library has sought to uphold this value, and has served as one of Baltimore's most venerable institutions. Growing from one branch in the city's business district to twenty-three locations in almost every community, the Pratt Library provides numerous community services beyond the traditional library function.[1] Since the 1990s, the Pratt Library has directed its focus on providing services and programs that address social inequities present in Baltimore, including employment training, educational programs for children, family activities that incorporate the city's rich multicultural background, technology training to address the digital divide, and workshops providing advice for small businesses. Program offerings have grown considerably within the last fifteen years in order to address Baltimore's changing demographics and its societal challenges. This chapter will discuss four successful library programs that, since the mid-1990s, have directly addressed social equity matters and contributed to the resilience and growth of Baltimore.

How do the functions of a public library system contribute to a resilient city? Resilience is the ability of a community to respond effectively to stress; and Baltimore has certainly experienced a myriad of stressful conditions and shocks over the past thirty years. Since the late 1950s, the city's population has declined from almost one million to approximately 621,000 in 2010.[2] From the late 1970s to the

Enoch Pratt Free Library, Baltimore, Maryland. Photo courtesy Enoch Pratt Free Library.

mid-1990s, Baltimore has suffered from disinvestment and an increase in crime stemming from the illegal drug economy. Through these circumstances, the efforts of the Pratt Library have provided critical resources to communities most affected: working-class city residents, at-risk populations, and minority groups. The library has sought to use its resources to assist these populations in a way that promotes resiliency, by enhancing learning capacity in the community through decentralized programming. These principles are present throughout all of Pratt's programs that address social equity.[3]

Seeds of innovation

The Pratt Library's programs run the gamut from literacy and general education programs for children, adolescents, and adults to family-oriented activities including health and wellness workshops and multicultural celebrations. It has also offered presentations that focus on everyday finances such as home-buying seminars, financial management, and income tax assistance, as well as employment and community economic development programming. The library's Business Center and the Job and Career Information Center both provide opportunities for patrons to learn how to start a business, to perform market research on what types of businesses would be suitable, and provide small business owner assistance and career and job search training.

Small businesses employ half of America's private sector workforce.[4] Therefore, support mechanisms are needed to assist small business owners with industry research, legal matters, and general business issues. As the Urban Libraries Council points out, awareness of this need has led to skill-building instruction for small business owners becoming a permanent component of public library programming.[5] This is certainly the case at the Pratt Library, where the Central Library's Business Center has operated for over ten years, annually providing substantial assistance to hundreds of aspiring and current small business owners. Services and resources include electronic database access for company and industry research, small business information workshops, and business and marketing plan assistance.

It has now become commonplace for many public libraries to institute career information centers in their branches.[6] The Pratt Library headed this trend, having operated its Job and Career Center since the mid-1990s. With the Job and Career Center located at the system's central location, the Pratt Library has developed a comprehensive program in place to assist patrons with their job-hunting and training efforts. In addition to housing a substantial collection of career- and job-related books and study guides for specialized training, the Job and Career Center also holds workshops on such skills as applying for a job online and résumé writing. The center also provides free résumé review by appointment.

Attendees at a recent Enoch Pratt Free Library program. Photo courtesy Enoch Pratt Free Library.

The Business Center and Job and Career Center may both be housed at Pratt's Central Library, but workshops on job hunting are available periodically at other branches, and remote access for databases and online access to Maryland-based job websites are offered through the website. To further its outreach efforts, the Pratt Library has begun using social media platforms: in addition to a Facebook page informing patrons of all programs taking place at the library, the Job and Career Center also has a Twitter account, which posts notices regarding the center's workshops as well as job searching and career advice.

Technology training for all

According to a 2010 study titled *Opportunity for All: How the American Public Benefits from Internet Access at U.S. Libraries* (for which the Pratt Library was presented as one of four case study sites), computer and Internet access have evolved into a core library service: as of 2009, nearly one-third of Americans fourteen years and older used a public library computer or a public library's wireless network to access the Internet.[7] Computer and Internet access are

Enoch Pratt Free Library, Southeast Anchor Library. Photo courtesy Enoch Pratt Free Library.

available at every branch, and computer training is available through the library's Pratt Centers for Technology Training (PCTT), which are housed in five locations that are able to serve every community in the city.

Provided in six-week components, introductory courses in Microsoft applications, typing, and Internet skills are offered for individuals with little (or zero) computer experience. For patrons whose skill level is beyond introductory courses, advanced sessions in Microsoft applications and other computer skills are available at the Southeast Anchor Library and the Orleans Street Branch. Additional targeted programs offered at the Orleans Street Branch that build even further on these skills include E-Portfolio (which enables job seekers to showcase their skills digitally), SeniorTech (aimed at patrons fifty-five years and older), and Kids Summer Computer Camp, which encourages computer literacy in children and adolescents.

PCTT FACILITY STATISTICS

Branch Location	Number of Computers at PCTT Facility	Computers Accessible to Individuals with Disabilities
Central Library	30	Yes
Northwood Branch	8	No
Orleans Street Branch	24	Yes
Pennsylvania Avenue Branch	12	No
Southeast Anchor Branch	24	Yes

Source: Enoch Pratt Free Library

From 2002 to 2008, the number of individuals participating in PCTT programs has risen from 6,000 to 75,000 per year, and in a typical year, over 500 classes are held teaching the skills necessary for career success in the twenty-first century. The PCTT promotes the availability of technological education opportunities in areas of the city where they might not otherwise be available, particularly for patrons unable to obtain such training due to financial barriers.

Preparing a new generation for work and service

In 1999, the Pratt Library began the Community Youth Corps (CYC) program to provide students from ages 13 to 16 with working experience in the library to enrich their employment preparation. The program is held for six months per cohort and participants receive a total of 25 hours of training, 15 of which are received prior to the student being placed at a library branch, and CYC participants are also able to accrue service-learning hours.[8]

The CYC has received financial support from outside organizations and from patrons. During the CYC's first three years of operation, the program was funded by a grant from the Wallace Foundation, a key objective of which was to provide opportunities to economically disadvantaged youngsters.[9] Originally operating at the Central Library and four branches, the CYC program was expanded at the end of the grant period to all of the library branches, based on its successful implementation. Today, the CYC is funded through various sources, including donors and patrons alike.

Applicants are given up to three choices of locations where they would like to work and are encouraged to choose locations near their school or home in order to ease the transportation burden of applicants or their parents. Once applicants are placed at a branch, they receive training in library and research skills, web page design, team building, and customer service. Corps members "shadow" librarians in clerical assistance, children's library activities, and reference activities. Corps members who work in branches with the Pratt Centers for Technology Training labs also assist lab staff with patron training sessions, technical troubleshooting, and in assisting patrons with online catalog and Internet searches. Since the CYC program began operating, hundreds of Baltimore City middle school and high school students have completed the program: between fiscal years 2004 and 2008, the program averaged 130 corps members per year, and numbers have recently increased to 224 and 235 participants in fiscal years 2009 and 2010, respectively.

Pratt's programming and services play a significant role in the local economy. Baltimore is in the beginnings of a workforce revitalization, with an increase of biotech companies and other technology incubator projects locating into the city. Companies in biotech and bioscience (and other) industries will need an educated workforce to draw from in the near future. The Pratt Library, in providing the skill-building programming and services described above, will surely assist many residents in obtaining these twenty-first-century jobs and may inspire the exploration of new careers. The Pratt Library has contributed and continues to contribute to Baltimore's resiliency by developing the city's human capital, and this support for an educated workforce will benefit Baltimore economically and socially for future generations, thus contributing to a sustainable, resilient city.

NOTES

1. This number includes the Central Library, an anchor library site, mobile library services and twenty branch libraries.

2. U.S. Census Bureau On-line Database, http://quickfacts.census.gov/qfd/states/24/24510.html.

3. Urban Libraries Council, *Partners for the Future: Public Libraries and Local Governments Creating Sustainable Communities*, http://urbanlibraries.org/associations/9851/files/0110ulc_sustainability_singlepages_rev.pdf: 23–27.

4. U.S. Small Business Administration, *The Small Business Economy—A Report to the President* (Washington, DC: U.S. Government Printing Office, 2009), 7.

5. Urban Libraries Council, *Making Cities Stronger: Public Library Contributions to Local Economic Development*, http://urbanlibraries.org/associations/9851/files/making_cities_stronger.pdf.

6. Ibid., 13–14.

7. Samantha Becker and others, *Opportunity for All: How the American Public Benefits from Internet Access at U.S. Libraries* (Washington, DC: Institute of Museum and Library Services, 2010), 1.

8. Middle and high school students in the state of Maryland are required to perform seventy-five hours of community service as a prerequisite for obtaining a state high school diploma.

9. Deborah Taylor, e-mail communication to author, January 5, 2011.

chapter five

Deborah Olley Murphy and Denise Clark

Queens Library's Literacy Zone Welcome Center at Long Island City

n 2009, Queens Library applied for funding from the New York State Education Department to establish a Literacy Zone in two high-needs Long Island City zip codes. Literacy Zones are defined by the New York State Education Department as

> a reform initiative to close the achievement gap in urban and rural communities of concentrated poverty and high concentrations of families and adults with limited literacy skills or English language proficiency. Literacy Zones are intended to provide a systemic focus in communities to meet the literacy needs of adults and families.[1]

Our purpose in applying for this grant was to augment our already well-established Adult Learning Center (ALC) in the Queens neighborhood of Long Island City with additional referral services, program workshops (financial, health, work, and art literacy), staff training, and materials for students in discussion groups. Ultimately, all English for Speakers of Other Languages (ESOL) students, as well as Adult Basic Education (ABE) students, would be offered health and financial literacy classes.

With Literacy Zone funding, Queens Library also sought to improve participants' lives, giving them a pathway out of poverty. This meant hiring a case manager to identify specific needs and partner agencies that would best serve each family. The case manager would help participants determine their eligibility for

Queens Library, Long Island City branch. Photo courtesy Queens Library.

benefits such as the Supplemental Nutrition Assistance Program (called SNAP, and formerly known as food stamps), Health Care Plus, and other health care benefits, earned income tax credits, and more. With assistance from the Literacy Zone, participants would get the help they needed to navigate complex and confusing health care, social services, education, and financial systems.

Needs assessment

When Queens Library applied for a Literacy Zone, the zip codes of 11101 and 11106 were ideal locations for the project for a number of reasons, as they house two of the largest public housing complexes in the United States, with more than 12,000 residents, many of them immigrants. Within these two zip codes, 32 percent of the population live below the poverty line, while 61 percent require public assistance to meet the health and nutritional needs of their families. In addition, 56 percent have Medicaid as their only form of health insurance. In Queens, the residents of Long Island City have significant educational, financial, and health needs: nearly 38 percent of the population have less than a high school diploma or GED, 57 percent are foreign-born, and 70 percent of children living in these zip codes are born to immigrants.[2] Queens Library already serves five schools within this community, at which an average of 76 percent of the students are eligible for free or reduced lunches.

In order to respond to the clear needs of this particular community, Queens Library also runs two family literacy centers in these zip codes: one in Queensbridge, and one in Ravenswood. The family literacy centers focus on the needs of parents/caregivers and their children, making learning a family affair. The second floor of Queens Library at Long Island City is dedicated to the Adult Learning Center (ALC), which provides one-on-one and group tutoring, classes, a computer lab, books and other learning materials, a conference room, a self-study area, and listening stations. The two family literacy centers and the ALC are within six blocks of each other. The main Welcome Center is located at the Jeanne Elmezzi ALC (Queens Library at Long Island City), while the annex is based at the Ravenswood Family Learning Center.

Lifelong learning at the Welcome Center

The Welcome Center at Queens Library takes a holistic approach to assisting its users, focusing on both educational and social services (outlined below). Building on the success of the Jeanne Elmezzi Adult Learning Center at Long Island City, it offers several levels of English for Speakers of Other Languages (ESOL) classes for adults, including classes for adult learners who are nonliterate in their native languages. The Welcome Center also reaches out to disenfranchised youth, ages 16–24, with pre-GED classes, as well as to adults reading below a fifth-grade level, with Adult Basic Education (ABE) tutorial groups. In addition, there are family literacy classes for families with pre-K children.

The Welcome Center uses established curricula and instructional practices under the aegis of the ALC, designed to develop reading, writing, and critical-thinking skills for all literacy students. Tutors work to identify the specific learning goals of each student, and use student-centered lessons that incorporate a balanced literacy approach—that is, the principles of whole language combined with specific skills instruction.

The Welcome Center also allows for independent learners and those users who would prefer to study on their own. The Jeanne Elmezzi ALC is fully equipped with hundreds of books and materials for ESOL and ABE learners. The ALC has videotapes available as well as audiobooks, and users can check books out. Learners can also choose to join the conversation group tutorials or small literacy groups.

At the Long Island City Welcome Center, users have access to eight desktop and sixteen wireless computers. Each computer is fully equipped with Internet access and educational software. The Welcome Center annex at Ravenswood has eight desktops and two laptop computers for testing and special presentations, including PowerPoint presentations and videos. Each site has conference rooms and meeting spaces.

Combining customer service with social service

The name given to the Literacy Zone, "Welcome Center," accurately reflects what the Queens Library is building within the Long Island City community—a central location where residents can come with a host of challenges and receive the assistance they so acutely need. New Americans are sometimes unsure of where to turn when they first arrive in the United States; they have no idea what services are available, and need to know what they can do to improve their own lives and the lives of their children.

Because the Welcome Center works in tandem with the Jeanne Elmezzi ALC at Long Island City and the Family Literacy Center at Ravenswood, it is ideally positioned to reach people in need. Through Queens Library's family literacy programs, much of the necessary groundwork for serving this population is already in place. Specifically, ALC staff first assesses who the participants are, where they are from, where they are now, and their goals for themselves and for their families. Because of an individualized intake process, ALC staff members can assess the social and work skills that participants need in addition to the educational classes they require.

Together with the Jeanne Elmezzi Adult Learning Center at Long Island City and the Family Literacy Center at Ravenswood, the Welcome Center helps people in the community to improve their education prospects and job skills, and also gets them real answers to their questions about health care, housing, nutrition, and more. According to Sandra Michele Echols, project coordinator/case manager for the project, "We're providing social service with customer service."

Since Queens Library already has established partnerships with several organizations in the area, the Welcome Center has been able to build on them to transition students of all ages (including those with learning disabilities) to employment, training, and further educational opportunities. These partners include the Department of Education, Workforce One Career Center, the City University of New York, and Vocational and Educational Services for Individuals with Disabilities. The Welcome Center has also built upon Queens Library's experience in working with post-incarcerated youth, through a partnership with the Vera Institute. And, in her role as case manager, Echols is able to follow through on referrals for people who use the Welcome Center, making sure they get the results they need.

Echols offers concrete examples of the Welcome Center in action. "If someone comes in with credit card debt and needs help," she says, "I not only can get them a referral to an organization such as the East River Development Alliance—I can monitor that referral. Or I can go online *with* the customer to apply for nutrition assistance or Medicaid." Echols explains that establishing partnerships with agencies is key, because for many people who are foreign-born and whose first language is not English, city agencies can be intimidating, and navigating these systems can be overwhelming.

On a Thursday morning, a class of nearly twenty women, most of them Bangla-speaking, attended a Welcome Center workshop on child care and learned about obtaining licensing for day care. A student named Rushna, who was attending the class and helping to translate the presenter's words into Bangla, said, "When this library opened, I came here and enrolled in the Adult Learning Center to learn English. I'm here today because I need a job." Another woman, Barkissa, who hails from Burkina Faso, explained that she had come to the class first and foremost for her own children. "I think this is a great opportunity for us," she said. "And the library does a lot for me. It's a place to learn and improve my English."

Queens Library is the only public library that is a lead agency for a Literacy Zone. Through this pilot project, we are providing our customers with trained staff and counselors who have the time and the expertise to sit down with people, find out what they need, and follow through with agencies.

Evaluation and assessment

Over the years, Queens Library has been a leader in lifelong learning, helping its customers with learning how to speak English, improving literacy, and assisting with job training. With the Welcome Center, we are building on our existing Adult Learner and Family Literacy programs, providing help to those who need it, strengthening families, and doing all we can to improve people's lives.

At the ALC, employees are able to track adult learners using its database. However, because the goals listed on the intake forms don't necessarily capture the same goals on which the Welcome Center is focused, and also because the database does not allow for capturing anecdotal information, the case manager keeps her own records.

Echols's monthly reports track users using specific categories, including case management services, training, and referral organizations. Over the span of a recent month, Echols served five walk-in customers, provided ongoing case management services to two people, and assisted individuals with referrals to vocational training programs and workforce organizations.

Over the first year of its grant, the Welcome Center served 85 people; the total goal, which Echols feels will be exceeded when the grant funding ends in 2012, is 365 users. Echols shared the following stories as anecdotal examples that the Welcome Center is making a difference in people's lives. When a young woman with chronic asthma who had aged out of her Medicaid benefits came to the Welcome Center, Echols assisted her in obtaining the medication she needed by helping her navigate the necessary websites. There was a woman from Burkina Faso who came to the Literacy Zone for child care training and has since become certified as a child care provider. Echols also displays a thank-you letter from a Haitian immigrant that features one key line: "In one afternoon," she wrote, "you single-handedly changed my life!"

When it comes to the future of the Welcome Center, Echols would like to see an outreach team formed, one focused on empowering local residents and connecting them with partners in the Long Island City area. She has an impassioned view of how and why the Welcome Center can have such far-reaching effects.

Echols insists that the key to eradicating poverty is adult education. While more and more venture philanthropists are investing in education at the K–12 level, she says, there is not enough money going into training the parents of these children. When parents don't have Internet access, when they are not educated themselves, says Echols, the children don't get the support they need at home to build on their education.

Queens Library is dedicated to sustaining the Welcome Center's success. When the grant funding from the New York State Education Department wraps up in June 2012, our intention is to incorporate this program into the high-quality ongoing programs and services we offer. While we will seek additional funding streams for the Welcome Center, we also will work to keeping the center open and operational for all of the public it serves. At the time of writing, the library has funding from two foundations and is currently awaiting word on two state funding applications.

Conclusion

Queens Library's Welcome Center is making a difference in the community, serving the educational and social service needs of an often disenfranchised public. Building on the success of our Adult Learner Program as well as our traditional reference services, the Welcome Center is reaching far beyond the confines of a traditional teacher-student relationship and assisting people with issues in their everyday lives—whether that is aid with nutrition and health care or finding work—in such a way that Queens Library is contributing significantly to community well-being. With the Welcome Center, we are not only fulfilling our mission of meeting the informational, cultural, and recreational needs and interests of our diverse and changing population, but we are truly enriching people's lives.

NOTES

1. New York State Education Department, 2011–2013 Literacy Zone Initiative: WIA Title II and Federal Adult Education and Family Literacy Act, www.p12.nysed.gov/funding/2011-13litzone/home.html.

2. U.S. Census Bureau, "U.S. Census' American Community Survey, 2007" (Washington, DC, 2007), www.census.gov/acs/www/.

chapter six

Monique Woroniak

From outreach to community development
Making sustainable choices at Winnipeg Public Library

T he immigrant population of Winnipeg, Manitoba, is significant and growing quickly. Between 1996 and 2000, only 15,809 new immigrants moved to the city; in the 2006 census 23,820 indicated they arrived in the city between 2000 and 2006, while a further 16,585 came in 2007–2008, and 9,910 in 2009.[1] Winnipeg is also home to a significant Aboriginal (i.e., First Nation/North American Indian, Metis, and Inuit) population. At 68,380 individuals, the Aboriginal peoples constitute 11 percent of the city's total population, giving Winnipeg the highest number of Aboriginal residents of any city in Canada.

Both the new immigrant and Aboriginal populations factor heavily into the work of the Winnipeg Public Library (WPL), and in particular its Outreach Services Unit. They are, of course, distinct from one another in terms of their history within the Canadian state, their languages and cultural traditions, educational needs, social support networks, and socioeconomic status. What they have in common, however, is that while many individuals within each of these groups may stand to benefit significantly from the services of a public library, barriers such as language, social exclusion, and no prior experience—or negative experiences—with public service agencies (including libraries) mean that targeted service strategies are often required.

This chapter will examine the above challenge as it relates to the WPL's tailored services for newcomers (i.e., new immigrants and refugees) and Aboriginal peoples, and will situate those efforts along a strategic continuum from outreach to community development service. An overview of outreach versus community development approaches and of the current funding context within which decision making takes place will demonstrate that, while a community development approach to service delivery is the optimal choice, the resources required can make this approach prohibitive. A key question to ask within an environment of limited resources is: what service delivery choices will result in a level of library service that is both of good quality (i.e., meets the needs of intended user groups) and sustainable?

The following four steps are put forward as a potential framework for answering the above question: first, recognize and acknowledge a service continuum based on the two poles of "outreach" and "community development"; second, set the goal of situating of services as close as possible to the community development pole; third, use comprehensive outreach efforts as a strategy to enable community development practices; and fourth, strive to develop and deliver community development services while still being sustainable within the operating context of the library system.

Overview: Winnipeg Public Library and outreach services

The Winnipeg Public Library serves a (2011) population of 663,617 and a metropolitan population of 730,018, of whom 373,452 are registered card holders.[2] The system is comprised of twenty branches, including the central Millennium Library. In addition, through its centralized Outreach Services Unit, the WPL provides monthly mobile library service to seventeen senior citizen residences and biweekly mobile library service, including programming, at two youth-focused sites in the inner city.

The Outreach Services Unit also assumes primary responsibility for the development and delivery of services tailored for newcomer and Aboriginal populations. The unit's staff complement includes two full-time outreach services librarians, each with a primary focus on either newcomer or Aboriginal communities. Three paraprofessionals primarily support the operation of mobile library services and the WPL's homebound library service.

Outreach services librarians participate in the development of new services in addition to working in a frontline capacity. The majority of programs are offered outside of WPL facilities in community centers, women's centers, newcomer organizations, Aboriginal support centers, and so on. The Outreach Services Unit also supports interactions with newcomers and Aboriginal peoples at the library branch level by arranging for tailored programming within branches and acting as a source of professional expertise for WPL staff.

System governance and funding

A recent Google search for "public libraries" and "budget cuts" returned 577,000 results. Not a scientific review of the landscape to be sure, but indicative all the same of the financial climate in which library systems are operating around the globe. While the Winnipeg Public Library does not operate in an austerity environment as extreme as many of our counterparts, it does face ongoing limits to its resources which necessitate highly strategic decisions to be made with respect to service delivery. Because the Winnipeg Public Library is a division within a municipal government department, it is primarily funded by the municipal government, which provides over 85 percent of total revenue. The current economic climate of fiscal restraint present in other North American cities has also manifested itself in Winnipeg. As of 2010 the city of Winnipeg maintained a thirteen-year freeze on property taxes and in 2009 levied the third-lowest amount of household property tax of fourteen Canadian cities with populations over 200,000. From 2008 to 2009 the WPL saw its number of full-time equivalent staff fall from 294 to 279. For context, in 2007 the WPL recorded 44 full-time equivalent positions per 100,000 population, which ranked its staffing levels among the lowest in Canada (compare with levels of 49 to 84 among five other medium and large cities).

Outreach versus community development

The need for outreach services to immigrant and Aboriginal populations is dramatic. The 2006 census recorded over thirty languages spoken in Winnipeg. Education attainment among Aboriginal residents is low compared to their non-Aboriginal counterparts: approximately 30 percent of Aboriginal residents have not completed secondary schooling, a rate that is more than double that of non-Aboriginal residents, and at slightly over 9 percent the unemployment rate among Aboriginal residents (aged 25–54) is nearly triple that of their non-Aboriginal counterparts.[3]

In its efforts to more effectively serve newcomer and Aboriginal populations, the WPL has had to make service development choices along the outreach–community development continuum. How do these two approaches differ? Canada's Working Together Project provides library-based definitions of both outreach and community development that have informed work at the WPL.[4] Initiated in 2004 and funded by Human Resources and Social Development Canada for four years, the Working Together Project piloted community development-based library initiatives in four urban Canadian library systems: Toronto, Vancouver, Regina, and Halifax.[5]

According to Working Together, the key difference between the outreach and community development approaches lies in where each situates the library in relation to the populations it seeks to serve. In an outreach approach the library retains its traditional position of expert and as an organization with a mission to deliver messages it believes are in the interest of healthy communities (e.g., support for early childhood literacy, lifelong learning, etc.). Outreach approaches are focused on an end—the delivery of a service that imparts a given message.

In a community development approach the library positions itself as a partner of the populations it seeks to serve. Community development-based service is focused on enacting a *process* of service development and delivery that is wholly based on partnerships with community members. Library services created through a community development approach employ much deeper collaboration than the consultative practices that typically inform outreach service. As a result, community development approaches result in services that are "user-driven" rather than "user-focused."

In an operational climate characterized in part by negligible revenue growth and periodic staff cuts, the WPL's decision making about service delivery for newcomer and Aboriginal populations has needed to be highly strategic. This has meant that initiatives have more often than not been informed by less demanding outreach approaches, as community development service requires significant amounts of staff time in order to establish—and, more importantly, to maintain—the necessary partnerships with community organizations and individual community members themselves. So while community development approaches have not always been feasible, they have remained an overarching service goal—an orientation that has informed the development of new services.

Outlined below are a select number of service initiatives undertaken since 2008 and tailored for either newcomer or Aboriginal populations. The majority of these initiatives reflect primarily an outreach approach, while several employ both outreach and community development service characteristics.

Revitalizing collections and programming for newcomers

In 2007 the WPL received grant funding to support collections of English-language learning materials for adult newcomers, dual-language storybooks for their children, and general adult literacy materials. The system built on the opportunity the new funds presented and chose to revitalize not only its collections for newcomers, but also its programming and general service delivery practices for that population. To that end, in 2008/2009 a major needs assessment regarding services for newcomers was designed and carried out by several librarians and a member of the WPL's administration. In addition to interviewing all library branch heads, section heads at the central Millennium Library, and key provincial government officials, library staff conducted interviews with numerous community practitioners, including English as an Additional Language (EAL) instructors, adult literacy instructors, and a number of adult literacy students themselves. Collections, library facilities, perceptions of service, marketing efforts, and programming were all included as lines of questioning, and the resulting report contained recommendations addressing all of these areas.

The decision to undertake the work of a needs assessment to inform how the grant monies were spent, in addition to garnering user feedback about other service areas, represented a strategic application of consultative work that situates the initiative solidly at the outreach end of the outreach–community development continuum. The process resulted in near-immediate augmentation and subsequent colocation of EAL and adult literacy materials at all twenty branches, and the decision to promote the materials under one banner—"Learning Collections." All these actions were informed by the needs assessment consultations.

New library programs informed by the needs assessment have included intergenerational story times for newcomers, most recently in the form of a "Moms and Tots" eight-week story-time session in partnership with a local newcomer organization. The format for this program was driven by the needs of group members as communicated by their instructor. Programming took place in a branch library and included a story time based on themes developed with the instructor over an extended period of time. Additionally, participants were provided with "read together" time for families to engage with dual-language and other relevant materials highlighted as part of the program. A weekly craft activity was included, and each session built in time for informal social exchanges among participants and with library branch staff. This program was well received and effective because its development was informed by a community development (user-driven) approach.

The program was ambitious in that it involved multiple sessions and incorporated several distinct components, undertakings which can seem daunting when weighing the amount of staff time required. In this case, a positive reception was virtually assured based on the fact that the program had been developed in partnership with those who were to receive its benefits. This program represents an example of a library service that benefited from the outreach work of a comprehensive needs assessment that itself was informed by user-driven practices—two factors which, combined, characterize the program as a blend of outreach and community development work. Preliminary discussions with individual participants themselves and a longer term for the program would likely have served to position the initiative closer to the community development end of the continuum. However, the program as executed did provide a high-quality, largely user-driven service which also has good potential for replication throughout the WPL system.

A related initiative for newcomers, and one that was also informed by the needs assessment, has been the development of a series of downloadable library orientation photo stories and activities. Like the "Moms and Tots" program above, this initiative was developed in partnership with EAL instructors and also employed the services of an immigrant community member in producing the final products.

The documents enable EAL practitioners and community members to learn practical information about the WPL (e.g., getting a library card, borrowing a book, due dates, finding EAL materials) through photographs of library use with captions and related activities for a range of English-language ability levels. Pedagogical approaches highlighted in the needs assessment (e.g., a focus on the visual, use of differentiated levels of English language) are found throughout the materials. The reception of these resources has been very positive—a result, again, of solid preliminary outreach work. While developing the documents required a considerable investment of staff time, the WPL could be assured of a certain degree of "payoff" because of the partnered, user-driven approach taken in developing the materials themselves. In addition, this initiative was of strategic, sustainable benefit to the library system because of its empowering effect on branch library staff, who now have access to relevant and effective orientation materials with which to better serve their local newcomer communities.

Revitalizing collections and programming for Aboriginal peoples

Similar to its recent initiatives related to newcomers, the WPL has also leveraged new funding to revitalize its services tailored for Aboriginal peoples. Once again the decision was made to employ a comprehensive needs assessment representing a major outreach-focused initiative on which to build new service delivery models. Most recently, the WPL (through its board) received funding from the city of Winnipeg's Aboriginal Youth Strategy (AYS) or Oshki Annishinabe Nigaaniwak—Young Aboriginal People Leading, which was put toward several initiatives, among which were a wide-ranging needs assessment conducted by a contractor with members of Aboriginal communities in the city; augmentation of the system's Aboriginal-language materials holdings; and the establishment of programming supported by an Elder-in-Residence.

Tabled in 2010, the "Needs Assessment and Report on Library Services with Aboriginal Populations Living in Winnipeg" was the result of extensive community consultations, which included interviews with fourteen leaders within major Aboriginal service organizations and schools, discussion circles with over 100 community members, and the completion of written surveys by over 130 community members.[6] As with the newcomer needs assessment, this document represents a foundation piece on which to grow future service initiatives with Aboriginal peoples in Winnipeg. While the needs assessment itself lies firmly on the outreach end of the continuum, the breadth of its lines of questioning and the depth of its consultations with community members themselves bode well for its ability to inform highly responsive and user-driven service initiatives.

Funding for the Aboriginal Youth Strategy also supported the purchase of significant amounts of Aboriginal-language and language-learning materials for both adults and children. Aboriginal languages and language-learning materials created at levels for the general public (i.e., as opposed to academic linguistics-based materials) are still sufficiently new and rare to make them a "hook" for engaging certain members of Aboriginal communities. This, along with the materials' inherent value in preserving and promoting Aboriginal languages and culture, was the rationale for this project. Materials were placed in the central Millennium Library and two branch libraries that had designated Aboriginal Resources Collections. (At the Millennium Library children's language materials were shelved in the library's signature Aboriginal Reading-in-the-Round children's collection and programming area. This unique space was itself the result of outreach-focused work pre-2005 when the central library was undergoing extensive renovations.)

Empirical data regarding the communities' perception and use of the WPL's Aboriginal-language materials have yet to be collected; however, library staff have found the presence of the materials to be an effective talking point about the system when interacting with community members.

Finally, another current Aboriginal-focused initiative at the WPL is the development of programming supported by an Elder-in-Residence (also funded by the City's AYS). The WPL received funding to support the costs of programming with a community Elder for 2010 and 2011. To date, programming facilitated with the Elder-in-Residence has included reading circles using Aboriginal-themed graphic novels; cultural teaching about themes such as naming ceremonies, clans, and personal colors; teepee teachings; sweat lodge teachings (though not actual sweat lodge participation); drum making and medicine pouch making (along with related teaching and ceremonies); and tours of the system's central Millennium Library. While the initial idea to work with an Elder was not directly community-driven, the resulting programming can be situated further toward the community development end of the continuum. This is in large part due to the Elder who, at the outset, insisted that programming not be pushed, in any way, on community members or community groups.

The practice at the WPL has been to reach out to community groups with a cursory overview of programming possibilities and to then request to meet with group leaders and—more important—group participants themselves. It is only after such meetings, or a series of meetings, take place that programming plans are developed. This type of program development requires significant investments of staff time due not only to the extensive user consultations but also to the fact that most programs are distinct from each other. A given group may be interested in medicine pouch making, while another only in online sources for cultural information, and another still in resources for women's entrepreneurship. While there have been some repeat requests, more often than not community members express an interest in information for which a program template has yet to be developed. The result has been a series of programs that have been very well received by users for the simple reason that the offerings were exactly what community members stated they either needed or wanted. As is characteristic of community development-focused work, the distance between practitioner and user was reduced dramatically—guesswork was largely eliminated and rich learning experiences for both parties resulted, including valuable staff knowledge that can be shared and utilized throughout the system.

Conclusion

In the current fiscal climate which, depending on geography, ranges from restraint to extreme austerity, public libraries are nonetheless as busy as ever. This is doubly true for libraries operating in communities that have significant populations requiring tailored services. And there, of course, lies both our rock (limited resources) and our hard place (users requiring extensive, meaningful contact with our organizations). What is a library system to do? It is this author's hope that the approaches and examples offered in this piece provide some useful direction. The approaches discussed were the result of decision making guided by the four steps laid out at the onset, namely that a library system

- familiarize itself with the differences between the concepts of "outreach" and "community development";

- establish community development-informed practices as the goal of library services offered;

- discover and take advantage of the catalytic qualities of comprehensive outreach work as they relate to even small, community development-focused interactions and projects; and

- situate the development and delivery methods of new services as near to the "community development" ideal as possible while enacting those services in a way that is sustainable given the limits to the library system's resources.

Because of the additional work and resources required by community development-focused services, it can be difficult to commit to the kind of decision making necessary to support the fourth step noted above. This is particularly true if staff have already taken part in even small amounts of community development-focused work. The rewards of such work, which include the sheer pleasure of witnessing community-driven library services benefit individuals directly, can make staff inclined to advocate for a community development approach to all projects. While this is a worthwhile and, per the steps above, necessary goal, what is not ideal is for a library system to head down a community development path for a time, only to have to dramatically (particularly from the perspective of community members) change tack when the system's resources can no longer support such resource-heavy initiatives.

In making incremental decisions along the way to community development-focused library service, the analogy of the sprint versus the marathon is useful. A public full of information needs, including those who require our services to be tailored to very specific life circumstances, will be with us for the long term. Library systems need to be strategic about their decision making to ensure that we are offering quality, meaningful services—but more important that we are able to offer these services in ways that will enable our users to count on us for the duration of their own journeys.

The good news is that, as outreach work can beget community development services, the latter can act as a catalyst for future community development-focused projects. Through strategic decision making, and despite climates of fiscal restraint, it remains possible for libraries to create tailored services for community members who arguably have the most to gain from engaging with our institutions.

NOTES

1. City of Winnipeg, *2006 Census Data—City of Winnipeg* (Winnipeg: City of Winnipeg, n.d.), http://winnipeg.ca/Census/2006/City%20of%20Winnipeg/City%20of%20Winnipeg/City%20of%20Winnipeg.pdf; Steve Lafleur, "Can the Winnipeg Model Save Detroit?" *New Geography,* May 15, 2011, www.newgeography.com/content/002238-can-winnipeg-model-save-detroit; Government of Manitoba, Manitoba Labour and Immigration, *Manitoba Immigration Facts—2009 Statistical Report* (Winnipeg: Labour and Immigration, 2009), http://www2.immigratemanitoba.com/asset_library/en/resources/pdf/manitoba-immigration-facts-report-2009.pdf.

2. City of Winnipeg, "Population of Winnipeg," www.winnipeg.ca/cao/pdfs/population.pdf.

3. Statistics Canada, *2006 Aboriginal Population Profile for Winnipeg,* cat. no. 89-638-X no. 2010003, Ottawa, 2010, http://dsp-psd.pwgsc.gc.ca/collections/collection_2010/statcan/89- 638/winnipeg-eng.pdf.

4. Working Together Project, "Outreach," *Libraries in Communities,* www.librariesincommunities.ca/?page_id=7.

5. Working Together Project, "Libraries in Communities Toolkit" (Vancouver: Libraries in Communities, 2008), www.librariesincommunities.ca/resources/Community-Led_Libraries_Toolkit.pdf.

6. Leskiw and Associates, "Needs Assessment and Report on Library Services with Aboriginal Populations Living in Winnipeg, Final Report" (2010), http://wpl.winnipeg.ca/library/pdfs/WPLBAboriginalPopulations.pdf.

With thanks to: Kathleen Williams, Winnipeg Public Library administrative coordinator of community outreach and marketing; Christopher Laurie, outreach services librarian; and the late Elder Betson Prince, Winnipeg Public Library elder-in-residence (2010, 2011).

Further Reading
City of Winnipeg, Community Services Department, Library Services Division, Great Community Spaces: 2010 Annual Report: Winnipeg Public Library (Winnipeg: City of Winnipeg, 2011), http://wpl.winnipeg.ca/library/pdfs/WPLannualreport10.pdf.

chapter seven

Melissa S. Rauseo and Julie Biando Edwards

Summer foods, libraries, and resiliency
Creative problem solving and community partnerships in Massachusetts

Providing food at library programs is not a new concept. Snacks are often a staple at children's story times, and it's a well-known idiom in Teen Services that "if you feed them, they will come." Many libraries are adding cafés and coffee carts to their services in order to both create a more welcoming physical location and to promote the library as a community gathering place. A summer lunch program allows libraries to move beyond using food to draw children and teens into the library for events and offer a vital service that helps enhance community food security and community resiliency.

As the catalyst for bringing a Summer Food Service Program (SFSP) to Peabody, Massachusetts, the Peabody Institute Library positioned itself as a strong community leader capable of identifying and bringing various partners to the table to address local food security and hunger issues. This chapter will use the Peabody Library's participation in the SFSP as an example of how libraries can support resilient cities and will argue that public libraries need to think beyond traditional library services when considering how best to meet the needs of communities.

Food security and insecurity in the United States

The United States Department of Agriculture (USDA) defines food security as

> access by all members [of a household] at all times to enough food for an active, healthy life. Food security includes at a minimum: the ready

availability of nutritionally adequate and safe foods [and the] assured ability to acquire acceptable foods in socially acceptable ways (that is, without resorting to emergency food supplies, scavenging, stealing, or other coping strategies).[1]

Each December, as a supplement to the Current Population Survey, about 50,000 households answer questions about food security, the amount of money they spend on food, and their use of federal or community food assistance programs. Answers fall along a continuum that includes the following categories: high food security, marginal food security, low food security, and very low food security. Within these categories households fall into a range of food insecurity severity extending from least severe to most severe. According to data from the 2009 survey, almost 15 percent of households were food insecure—an estimated 50.2 million people, including 17.2 million children.[2]

Issues of food security and insecurity are not limited to individual households, but ripple into the community. As such, strategies to address them must be appropriately broad. The USDA describes community food security as

- a prevention-oriented concept that supports the development and enhancement of sustainable, community-based strategies:
- to improve access of low-income households to healthful nutritious food supplies,
- to increase the self-reliance of communities in providing for their own food needs, and
- to promote comprehensive responses to local food, farm, and nutrition issues.[3]

Community food security programs have the potential to address a number of local issues ranging from food availability and affordability to job security and community development. While libraries certainly cannot address all of the circumstances that lead to individual households being food insecure, they can (and we believe should) play a role in addressing community food security, in association with community partners. As both sources of information and as community-based institutions, libraries can contribute to many aspects of a food-secure community. By creating partnerships with other local institutions, libraries can both address some of the causes of food insecurity and help create social cohesion, one of the issues listed by the USDA as an aspect of community food security and one of the markers of a resilient community.

Background: Peabody Institute Library

The Peabody Institute Library sits at the heart of downtown Peabody, Massachusetts. A community of approximately 50,000 with a thriving past in leatherworking, Peabody is suffering—like many former industrial centers—from economic restructuring that closed mills and factories. In recent years local government has worked on strengthening the city's economy and revitalizing the community. Peabody is a richly diverse city with a strong multicultural heritage developed throughout the twentieth century. Founding families that stretch back to colonial times, as well as residents of Greek and Portuguese ancestry, live alongside new neighbors who have recently immigrated from Brazil and the Dominican Republic. Community pride is strong in Peabody and the local government, of which the library is a part, is keenly interested in the economic and social revitalization of the downtown area in particular.

The library was founded in 1852 when George Peabody, a locally raised, self-made businessman who found enormous success and wealth as an investment banker in London, donated $20,000 toward what would be called the Peabody Institute. The institute was to be both a library and a lyceum (a hall where concerts or educational lectures are presented) and, unlike similar facilities at the time, would be free and open to the public. An active, generous, and wide-ranging philanthropist, Peabody gave over $217,000 to the Peabody Institute by the time he died in 1869. In creating the institute, Peabody paid homage to his hometown and to the opportunities it had presented to him. His express wish, outlined in the letter that accompanied the initial $20,000 gift, was simply that the institute exist to meet the informational, educational, and recreational needs of local citizens. In many ways, the vision that Peabody bequeathed to the institute was as important as the financial support he provided; and, over a century later, the Peabody Library continues to commit itself to its founder's ideals, owning as its mission the simple but profound goal of meeting the "informational, educational, and recreational" needs of its community.

While the mission of the Peabody Library has remained unchanged since 1852, the ways in which the library meets that mission have changed significantly. Today the Peabody Library understands its mission to be best carried out through a wide variety of programming, outreach, and community building. Both library administrators and librarians enthusiastically support and promote programming opportunities, and as a result there is not a week, and often not a day, that goes by without at least one program scheduled. Often there are several—concerts, book clubs, story hours, craft workshops, cooking classes, art classes, teen drop-in hours—going on at once, and it is not unusual for all library meeting rooms to be booked at the same time.

Librarians in Peabody make it a priority to partner with others when creating or designing programs and routinely reach out to create partnerships with local institutions, schools, and clubs in order to best meet the needs of a wide variety of patrons. Similarly, librarians have made it a priority to make programming visible. Good working relationships with local media outlets provide a forum for advertising and reporting, and librarians very often take programming out of the building. We have hosted numerous programs at City Hall, and the children's and young adult librarians often host summer reading programs and concerts with local teen bands on the lawn outside. Passersby on Main Street can't help but notice goats on the library lawn, or a sound system set up for a local rock group. This commitment to programming and outreach has made the library a focal point of the community. Indeed, helping create community is a top priority for the library, which understands that the creation of community is implicit in George Peabody's vision. This commitment to all members of the community has benefited both the library, which is seen as a proactive and dynamic city entity, and the city itself.

Located in the center of downtown, in an urban and low-income location, the library routinely sees the needs of the community, including those of its youngest members, at firsthand. In recent years, librarians have noticed that more and more children are at the library for the entire day in the summer, or from after school until closing during the school year. Always seeking proactive, community-minded approaches to meeting people's needs, and realizing that children and teens have found in the library a safe place in which to spend time, Peabody's librarians have set up a variety of programs and spaces for young patrons. For example, the Young Adult Drop-in Area, supported by grants and the occasional donation of materials and electronics, was explicitly set up to provide a place for teens to congregate in the absence of a local youth center, to access a TV and video games, crafts, and snacks.

As children and young people spend many hours a day utilizing the library as a safe space, librarians began to notice that many of the young people in our community were going long periods of time without eating, especially in the summer. Many of them relied on the local soup kitchen for dinner six nights a week, but other meal sources were less reliable. Though this could be read as a social services issue and not a library one, librarians at Peabody were understandably concerned about the fact that so many children and young adults might be going hungry. While the library could not single-handedly feed hungry members of the community, the librarians realized that they could take steps toward creating a programming partnership that could make a significant contribution.

Summer food service programs and public libraries: a growing partnership

During the 2009 school year, 31.3 million children nationwide received free or reduced lunches through the National School Lunch Program (NSLP), which is funded by the USDA.[4] The NSLP has been in existence since 1946 and provides lunches to low-income children nationwide. When school is out for the summer, however, many children lose this consistent source of nutritious food. In 1968, the USDA attempted to fill this gap in services through a pilot program that, in 1975, became the Summer Food Service Program, or SFSP. The SFSP provides free meals to children in low-income areas during the summer months, thus establishing year-round service of nutritious meals for children who might otherwise be hungry when school is not in session.[5]

The SFSP meals are overseen by local sponsors, most often a public school district, a city or town government, or a nonprofit organization, who secure or prepare the meals. Sponsors are responsible for reporting the number of meals served to a designated state agency in order to receive reimbursement. In Massachusetts, sponsors report to the Department of Elementary and Secondary Education, which receives funding for the SFSP from the Food and Nutrition Service, an agency of the USDA. Once a sponsor is secured, the free meals are served in local communities at sites hosted by a wide array of community organizations including schools, churches, and parks.

There are several types of sites that may serve meals through the SFSP. Most commonly, sites are either "open" or "enrolled." Open sites serve meals to any child, eighteen years of age or younger, who comes to the site. No enrollment or identification is required and, in addition to meals, many open sites provide free activities for participating children. Sites are eligible to be "open" based either on their location in a low-income census tract or on their proximity to a school that enrolls a high number of low-income children. Enrolled sites are ones in which meals are served to a set number of children, who are preenrolled for a structured program. In order for a program to qualify as an enrolled site, at least half of their children must be low income.

Nationally, the USDA has stated that the SFSP would be more successful in reaching low-income children if more community locations became feeding sites. Many parks and recreation departments have stepped forward and partnered with the SFSP in order to feed the children who attend their camps and summer programs. Like recreation departments, public libraries draw children and teens during the summer months, making them an attractive venue for the program. In addition to libraries in Peabody and San Diego (the original inspiration for the SFSP program in Peabody), other libraries are beginning to sign on as summer food sites. In Pulaski County, Kentucky, children can get lunch both at the library and from the library's bookmobile. This is a particularly beneficial partnership since transportation is one of the major issues facing rural communities who want to participate in the SFSP. The Yuma County Library in Arizona has also become a feeding site, and by adding a summer food program to their existing Summer Reading Program they registered over 1,000 children for summer reading the first year and almost 2,000 in the second year of the partnership. Both Pulaski and Yuma County Libraries have been recognized by the Food Research and Action Center as "model" summer food programs.

In July 2009, 2.8 million children nationwide were fed each weekday through the summer nutrition programs. This number, while great, represents only a small portion of the number of children who receive free or reduced lunches during the school year: it was estimated in 2009 that just one in six low-income schoolchildren were served by SFSP.[6]

Summer foods in Peabody

The inspiration for setting up the SFSP at the Peabody Library came from an article in the October 2008 issue of *American Libraries* by Jennifer Burek Pierce, describing the San Diego Public Library's involvement with the SFSP.[7] Peabody's young adult librarian approached the library's administration about the possibility of offering something similar as part of our summer programming schedule. Always keen to try new programs, we agreed that the idea was worth investigating.

As we learned more about the structure and requirements of the SFSP, it quickly became clear that a community partnership would be necessary to put something this large in place. When the library director brought the idea to a meeting of city department heads, the mayor strongly supported starting a summer feeding program within the city, and with his backing, the library organized a meeting with potential partners, including the public school system's Food Service Department, the Parks and Recreation Department, the Healthy Peabody Collaborative, and a local church. These original parties were selected by library staff based on their past participation and interest in community projects benefiting youth.

The first order of business was to find a sponsor and vendor for the SFSP meals. In many cities and towns, the public school's Food Service Department acts as both the sponsor and the vendor. During the initial meeting it became clear that this would not be a viable option for Peabody. The USDA's reimbursement rate for meals served would not be enough to cover the Food Service Department's expenses for staffing, food purchasing and preparation, and transportation. This seemed like an insurmountable obstacle until the city's Council on Aging volunteered to prepare and transport all the summer meals. Although not originally identified by the library as a potential partner, the council was able to work with the reimbursement rate because they already prepare meals at the Senior Center through another USDA feeding program. Their staffing costs were less, they utilized volunteers heavily, and they already had transportation in place through their Meals on Wheels program.

With the Council on Aging willing to act as the vendor for meals, the Healthy Peabody Collaborative (HPC), which builds community partnerships in order to create a healthier overall community, agreed to become the sponsor for Peabody's program. As the sponsor, they handled all the reporting and financial aspects of the SFSP. With a vendor and a sponsor secured, various potential feeding sites were considered. In the end, the city of Peabody had two SFSP sites in the summer of 2009. Because the library is located in a low-income census tract, it was qualified to be an open site that would feed any child under eighteen. The second site was at a local elementary school that offers a summer school program for young Spanish-speaking children. This program operated as a closed site that served meals only to its regular participants. HPC staff attended extensive training sessions given by the Massachusetts Department of Elementary and Secondary Education and, in turn, trained workers at the SFSP sites.

The new "Library Lunches" program ran four days a week for six weeks. The library's community room was open for an hour and a half each day, serving food. Since sites that have activities and events attract larger numbers of children, both the USDA and Project Bread, a leading hunger organization in Massachusetts that supports summer food programs, encourage sites to offer activities for children in conjunction with lunch. As a new site in 2009, the library was able to secure grant funding from Project Bread to buy supplies and equipment for both the food service aspect of the program and for activities. Our children's librarian purchased books, puzzles, games, coloring books, crayons, blocks, and hula hoops for "Library Lunch" participants.

Given our strong programming focus, we were keen to offer activities as part of "Library Lunches," but since the SFSP was running in addition to our usual summer programs for children and young adults, we knew that we would need volunteers to help with both the meals and with the activities at the lunch programs. Several community organizations were very enthusiastic about helping out, and the Healthy Peabody Collaborative agreed to coordinate all the volunteers. Volunteers from a local church came once a week to offer a variety of programs on subjects like knitting and gardening, and the pastor of this church also ran a special, weeklong art class. The Peabody Rotary Club sponsored a craft project and sent members to run the event, while other community volunteers (including a number of teens) played games and did other less-structured activities with the younger children.

The library's strong working relationship with the local media paid off, as many of the individual volunteers stepped forward to help after reading about the program in the newspaper. Help also came from some unexpected sources. A group of middle-school boys who were regular library patrons and ate lunch at the SFSP every day started helping to break down the tables and chairs and clean up at the end of the program. They were enthusiastic helpers and seemed pleased to be able to contribute to the library in a positive way.

Volunteers helped tremendously in making this program a success, but library staff also stayed involved in the SFSP. Because library staffing levels are often tight in the summer months due to staff vacations, our young adult librarian sought funding from our local Workforce Investment Board to hire a student worker through their program designed to help young adults find their first job. The young woman hired and supervised by the young adult librarian and Healthy Peabody Collaborative staff worked at the site every day, accepting and counting the meals when they were delivered, handing out lunches, keeping records, and generally monitoring the site.

The Peabody Library served 940 lunches during our six-week program in 2009. We averaged about forty children and teens at lunch each day, and while those numbers exceeded our expectations, Peabody's Summer Food Program, like most other programs in the country, only reached a tiny fraction of the youth who receive free and reduced lunches during the school year. The Peabody Library plans to improve our program in future years in a variety of ways, including better integrating our summer programs with the food program and expanding our marketing of the program.

The SFSP in Peabody went more smoothly than we could have imagined, and we had few issues and many successes. Parents and grandparents who regularly brought children to the program were enthusiastic and grateful. Volunteers found themselves in mentoring roles with the children whom they met through the lunches. One volunteer who works across the street from the library came to the lunch program to show kids how to knit. This volunteer worked very closely with one young woman who has special needs and, in the end, the volunteer told the young woman she could stop by her office anytime if she needed help with her knitting. Similarly, some of our middle-school youth who came regularly for lunch and to play games connected with a volunteer from the Sheriff's Department. This volunteer came to deliver an anti-drug message, but he had also written a children's book and would give copies to youth who won the board games they would all play together. So, while the initial objective was to feed kids who might not get a nutritious meal otherwise, the benefits ultimately extended beyond well-fed kids and into less tangible successes.

Summer food, libraries, and resiliency

While feeding hundreds of needy kids is certainly a significant success in itself, it's these less tangible successes that really point to the ways in which libraries can support resilient communities, by positively affecting both individuals and organizations in the community, addressing social issues, and creating lasting change. In fact, the creation of positive partnerships between individuals and organizations in the community is a key element in building resilient cities. In this section we will look at specific resiliency principles and how they relate to the SFSP experience in Peabody.

Self-organization

While certainly food security needs to be a feature in any resilient city or town, it is really the collaborative organization of the SFSP at the Peabody Library that makes it a model for libraries seeking to participate in building resiliency in their communities. We saw a need in our community, found a possible solution, and brought the necessary people together to make it happen. The library's existing community connections made it possible to innovate and problem solve in order to make the idea of a summer feeding program a reality. When it became clear that our School Food Services Department could not sponsor and vend our lunch program, library staff reached out to partners we had collaborated with in the past. The library director serves on numerous committees within the city and, through her connections, she was able to bring the Council on Aging to the table as a vendor. The young adult librarian works closely with the Healthy Peabody Collaborative and consequently was able to bring them on board as the sponsor. Throughout their sponsorship, the Healthy Peabody Collaborative proved to be a cornerstone of the project.

Once the library brought together the SFSP partners, each group utilized its strengths to create a program that benefited the youth of Peabody. The Healthy Peabody Collaborative leveraged its administrative skills and network of volunteers; the Council on Aging built upon an existing program of meal preparation and transportation; the library provided a physical location and offered our marketing, grant writing, and programming skills; and the local church tapped into its membership to find volunteers willing to share their time and talents with youth. In other cities and towns, the players will undoubtedly be different, but the need to create networks to meet community needs and overcome obstacles will be the same.

Public libraries are often a nexus for community collaborations, and the Peabody Library was one for the SFSP. The existing good relationships we had with other community organizations made this collaboration relatively easy in our case, as did the library's reputation for innovative services and programs. Our community partners wanted to be involved and eagerly participated by bringing their strengths to the table. This collaboration allowed us to create a program that would have been far too big for any one organization to run, and it illustrates the best kind of grassroots organizing. Libraries, particularly the best public libraries, have survived by being innovative and creating their own opportunities and resources. As an experienced librarian once told us, much of our job involves spinning straw into gold. This kind of self-organizing and coalition building—spearheaded by public libraries—can address community issues in ways that are often more immediately responsive, more innovative, and more adaptable than traditional bureaucratic methods involving committees or task forces.

Flexibility and adaptability

The Peabody Library staff did not enter into this program without reservations. We wanted to ensure that the food program didn't disrupt our regular services, and we were especially concerned about unattended children not being properly supervised. While the library is comfortable with its role as a community center, staff also recognized that this program might be crossing over into providing social services that are outside the library's mission. However, our reservations were tempered by a willingness to experiment.

Libraries and the SFSPs are more obvious partners than may appear at first glance. Most public libraries offer some type of summer reading program for youth. The logic behind these programs has long been that students who read during the summer will perform better when they return to school. Librarians promote summer reading programs as helping mitigate students' "summer learning loss." It is likewise recognized that summer feeding programs can help low-income students academically during the school year. The USDA's Food and Nutrition Service reports that students who do not receive adequate nutrition throughout the summer months don't perform as well once school restarts.[8] By combining a strong summer reading program with the SFSP, librarians can position themselves as important community partners in overall youth development.

Many public libraries already commit themselves to large, well-run summer reading programs. Often these programs rely on community partners for support with prizes or programs, so taking the next step to develop an SFSP could be seen as merely an extension of existing summer reading programs. In some ways, libraries won't need to create the SFSP from the ground up—they can build on what they have already found to be successful. The ability to look at an old program in a new way, or to use an existing program or service as scaffolding for something bigger and more far reaching, is something at which many public libraries are expert and can allow them to tackle a program that might otherwise have proved too daunting. This ability to reassess services and programs creatively and to tack on to them, build them up, or adjust them to fit a specific need is a key element in library and programmatic resiliency, particularly for libraries that may find themselves facing uncertain economic or political climates.

Decentralization and loosened interconnections

By including multiple community partners, the SFSP not only met a community need that contributed to making the city of Peabody more resilient, but also became a resilient program in its own right. In 2010, the Peabody Library underwent a major construction project to replace its heating, ventilation, and air conditioning (HVAC) unit. The construction shut down large sections of the building and, though the library remained open to the public and retained its most basic services (reference, circulation, access to public computers and so on), most library programming could not take place. Since we had to move the Reference Department and public computers into our community room, we had no place to run the SFSP.

Although the library was unable to act as a site for the SFSP in 2010, the program still operated. The responsibility for the program was decentralized enough that other partners were able to adjust to this change and ensure that the youth of Peabody still had a summer lunch program. The Healthy Peabody Collaborative worked with a local elementary school that runs a summer school program to create an alternative open-site location. The Council on Aging continued to vend the meals, and many of our volunteers, including the local church, stepped up again to help offer activities. The library stayed involved in the program by sending our young adult librarian to the school as a weekly volunteer.

While the HVAC construction project ran into the summer of 2011, the library, with the help of even more community partners, was able to host "Library Lunches" on a reduced scale. Library staff and patrons are looking forward to running a full-scale SFSP again, but the experiences of 2010 and 2011 have proven that the coalition the library brought together is a resilient one. The program itself is flexible, as are all the partners. The library takes great pride in the SFSP, but ownership is a shared endeavor. Territorialism can damage programs and do serious harm to collaboration, congeniality, and resiliency. The goal with the SFSP was not to create a library program, but rather to create a community program that was *spearheaded* by the library. This difference is subtle, but essential in creating resiliency. Pulling in multiple collaborators and encouraging them to use their best skills, as opposed to just seeking financial partners, meant that when the library had to step back for a year, others could step forward and the program would run seamlessly. It also meant that the individual partners were able to be resilient in a way that none of them might have imagined. By working together on a project too big for any one agency or institution, these organizations learned that they have what it takes to create a successful community service, even when the circumstances around the delivery of that service change.

Building and modeling resiliency

Public libraries are nothing if not adaptable, although one of their great beauties is their ability to blend adaptability with stability. We would argue, in fact, that this is exactly what a library should do, and that this model of library service is the best way to build resilient community and institutions.

Institutions like public libraries are perhaps the most aware of the varied needs of a community, and we believe that libraries should work, within their missions, to address community needs wherever possible. We would argue that libraries have a social responsibility to help the community recognize and address social problems. This is not to say, of course, that librarians should be social workers, or that libraries have the sole responsibility of addressing community needs. In fact, so many of the issues that communities face *cannot* be solely addressed by libraries, nor should they be. However, when the library notices a significant social problem in the community, it may be in a unique place to *bring attention to that problem* and, in some cases, to work with others to address that problem. In the case of the SFSP in Peabody, it was the library that raised the issue of hungry kids with City Hall, spearheaded the task of coalition building, and worked to develop a program that was influenced by but independent from the library. The end result was a sustainable, successful program that addressed a community need.

Adopting an agenda of building community resilience by taking the lead in addressing social needs also highlights the library as a resilient institution in its own right. Libraries have to be eminently adaptable and flexible, particularly in the face of budget cuts, reductions, and closures. A good public library will constantly be looking for new ways to demonstrate its worth to the community and to situate itself at the center of its community. In the past, the value of a library rested primarily in its collections. This may no longer be the case for most libraries, for which programming and services are becoming increasingly important. We suggest that the ability to help the community address its social needs will also become more important as well.

Public libraries have an opportunity to show our communities what it means to be adaptable, collaborative, and flexible. Libraries that are creative enough to find innovative ways to tackle problems, politically savvy enough to build coalitions, and flexible enough in their understandings of themselves will model resiliency in a very real way. They will continue to find new ways to highlight their value and to prove their worth to their communities. Without sacrificing the stability that the institution has always represented, we will be able to adapt to the wonderful, dynamic, sometimes scary fluctuations of our communities. In being resilient, we will help those around us learn to be so as well.

NOTES

1. U.S. Department of Agriculture, Economic Research Service, *Food Security in the United States: Measuring Household Food Security*, 2009, www.ers.usda.gov/briefing/foodsecurity/measurement.htm.

2. Mark Nord, Alisha Coleman-Jensen, Margaret Andrews, and Steven Carlson, *Household Food Security in the United States*, 2009, www.ers.usda.gov/Publications/ERR108/ERR108.pdf.

3. U.S. Department of Agriculture, Economic Research Service, *Food Security in the United States: Measuring Household Food Security*, 2009, www.ers.usda.gov/briefing/foodsecurity/measurement.htm.

4. U.S. Department of Agriculture, *National School Lunch Program Fact Sheet*, 2010, www.fns.usda.gov/cnd/lunch/aboutlunch/NSLPFactSheet.pdf.

5. Gordon W. Gunderson, *The National School Lunch Program: Background and Development*, U.S. Department of Agriculture, Food and Nutrition Service, 2009.

6. Food Research and Action Center, *Hunger Doesn't Take a Vacation: Summer Nutrition Status Report 2009* (Washington, DC: Food and Research Action Center 2009), http://frac.org/wp-content/uploads/2009/09/summer_report_2009.pdf.

7. Jennifer Burek Pierce, "Youth Matters: Feeding the Whole Child," *American Libraries* (October 2008): 68.

8. U.S. Department of Agriculture, Food and Nutrition Service, *Summer Food Service Program,* www.fns.usda.gov/cnd/summer/.

chapter eight

Mary Wilkins Jordan

Public library gardens
Playing a role in ecologically sustainable communities

Many communities are investing in gardens and green spaces in an effort to help their citizens connect with and experience nature. Research has shown that the amount of green spaces (or "vitamin G") in a community is connected with the perceived health and well-being of the members of that community.[1] Whether in regard to learning ability, early childhood development, community building, or reducing crime and the fear of crime, research has demonstrated the many positive impacts of green spaces, particularly for low-income urban residents, many of whom are otherwise often "nature-deprived."[2] Emphasizing the seriousness of this issue, Richard Louv's book *Last Child in the Woods: Saving Our Children from Nature-Deficit Disorder* has inspired legislators at both the federal and state levels to push for legislation called No Child Left Inside.[3] These pieces of legislation are aimed at encouraging children (and parents and schools) to get outside in green spaces, as they help to reduce levels of attention-deficit disorder and obesity in children, as well as contribute to the health and well-being of all members of a community.

The difficulty lies in creating and nurturing green spaces and gardens in communities in public places, not just in private yards. Setting up green spaces in places where people will actually go to see them is potentially tricky; gardens available in places community residents are already likely to visit would be ideal. Green spaces and growing gardens and other sorts of nature connections are not going to be useful to a community unless they are easily available to people. Public libraries provide an ideal situation for this connection.

Gardens and green spaces serve many important needs for communities: as a source of fresh fruits, vegetables, and herbs to address community food security needs; as a source of physical activity which may promote health and relaxation; as an important linkage with nature in an urban setting; and as a source of beauty for gardeners and the community as a whole. Public gardens, like libraries, are also key public spaces; it therefore makes sense for libraries looking for new and useful ways of connecting with their communities to establish library gardens. This combination can serve an educational role in helping members of the community learn more about gardening and nature.

Libraries across the country are already providing their communities with a wide variety of gardens: on rooftops, flower gardens, indoor gardens, vegetable gardens providing food to homeless shelters, demonstration gardens, and more. Looking at some of these gardens, and providing some suggestions for gardens in other libraries, reveals some of the innovative ways in which libraries are contributing positively to resiliency in their communities.

Background

To prepare for this research, the author distributed a posting to the PUBLIB electronic discussion list to solicit information from those libraries across the country that had operated or were currently managing publicly accessible gardens, both indoor and outdoor. Librarians were invited to submit information on their library's garden and to share information on other libraries they knew of that had gardens. Thirty libraries participated in this survey, but there are likely many more library gardens to be found in every state. The information below is derived from the responses received.

Only about half of the respondents to the survey answered the question of how old their library gardens were, but gardens seem to have generally been relatively new to most libraries. Twelve of them were started in the last five years, six were started between five and ten years ago, and three of them were begun more than ten years ago. The oldest garden was the Downtown Reno branch, Washoe County Library, built in 1966 when the building was constructed. Three of these thirty gardens have been started in the last year, indicating a possible increase in the awareness of the benefits of a library garden. That so many libraries have sustained their gardens over time, as was reported in this survey, is also a positive sign that library gardens are seen as worthwhile.

Why create a garden? So many reasons!

There were a wide variety of reasons reported for the creation of a garden in a library. The most common seems to be that an opportunity had presented itself: the library was constructing a new building, or doing a renovation project on their existing building. Adding a garden to a purpose-built space could then be done as part of the planning process, and would help to make the architect's designs even more inviting. Other library gardens have developed from a stated desire to contribute to common green spaces and green environmental practices.

Gardens integrated in a library building can be a significant contributor to "green" building objectives. The rooftop garden at the Addison, Illinois, public library, which covers about 30 percent of the total roof space, not only enhances an architecturally lovely building, but it serves as a rainwater abatement system and helps to reduce heat transfer in the hot summer months, a useful function of many rooftop gardens. Other gardens may be a way to help meet the community's needs for natural areas or demonstration spots for different community-based ecological practices, which give patrons (and others) the chance to see these practices in action. For example, the Grand Rapids (MI) Public Library had an environmental plan for their library but wanted to find ways to enhance it and use it to make more connections with the community. In response to a contest asking for ways to make the library a greener place, a staff member suggested a rain garden. Plans were quickly assembled to bring a garden to an area with standing water after rainfalls. The garden was officially opened on April 22, 2008, as part of the Earth Day celebration in the library. In Highland, California, the Sam J. Racadio Library & Environmental Learning Center set up their garden to be a part of their specialty environmental learning center in the library. The Mid Columbia Library in Kennewick, Washington, was built on a corner of land that was donated to be a 26-acre city park. A local university's master gardener asked the library for use of a piece of their land to serve as a demonstration garden. Permission was granted and the garden was built.

Several libraries developed their gardens in partnership with a local organization. At the Kenosha Public Library in Wisconsin, a former employee contacted the city's Keep Kenosha Beautiful program to discover what kinds of partnerships were available for the library locations. A coordinator from the city supplied the plants, mulch, and some other necessary items, and volunteers from the library provided the labor to keep the gardens blooming with flowers. Among responding libraries, Kenosha seems to be unique in having gardens in at least three different library locations in the city: a garden is kept blooming at their administration building; the main library has a garden site, developed when the new building was constructed; and their large Northside branch also has a garden of their own. Staff members at each location organize their own planting and provide the necessary labor to keep the gardens going.

It does take a certain amount of regular labor to keep up a garden, and libraries have different choices they can make about who specifically will handle that task. Most of the gardens in this survey use volunteer library staff labor in their gardens. Others use community volunteers, or a combination of staff and community members. A few pay landscapers to maintain the garden, and a few others use local community organizations to maintain the garden. The Zion-Benton Public Library garden is maintained by the Illinois Dunesland Garden Club. The garden in the Mid Columbia Library is maintained by the WSU Extension Service Master Gardener program. And the University City Public Library

(Missouri) reports they pay about $3,000 annually to the City in Bloom program, which provides volunteer assistance along with some paid staff. The money also helps to pay for the annual planting materials needed for the garden.

Those libraries that use volunteer help report a variety in the range of amounts of time it takes to maintain the garden. Generally, it does not seem to involve an overwhelming commitment of time and energy—a few hours a week, which is spread over a number of people—staff and volunteers. Watering and weeding are the tasks that seem to take the most time in the garden. This may be exacerbated by a lack of storage or other facilities for working with gardens or landscaping. The challenges involved in continued operation of a library garden should be considered prior to starting in on this project, but should not dissuade libraries from considering a garden of their own.

Some libraries encountered some issues in getting volunteers lined up prior to setting up the garden, as well having sufficient people in place for working in the garden long-term, as some of the early volunteers may not be able to follow through on their commitments or may not be motivated to keep coming back to the garden regularly.

At the University City Public Library, the City in Bloom program set up the garden at the library. Later that garden was improved beyond the original conception. The Whitestone Community Library, Queens Library garden is a collaborative project between the library and the Horticultural Society of New York. In addition, the library received grant money to make their vision of a garden come alive for their community. The Community Library in Salem, Wisconsin, set up their library garden in conjunction with their local Girl Scout troop, providing not only a beautiful garden for community residents, but also a good way to help the Girl Scouts learn about gardening practices.

Memorial gardens have a long history, and some libraries have established gardens to honor a person connected to that institution. The Zion-Benton Public Library, north of Chicago, established their garden to memorialize a former library trustee and a member of the Illinois Dunesland Garden Club. At the Rochester (NY) Public Library garden, money was donated in memory of the daughter of their then-president of the board, as a planned gift project to start their library garden.

The basics of good gardens

As anyone who has worked in a garden knows, gardens require planning and labor, as well as a strategy for maintaining the garden after it is established. In the case of a public garden, these activities in turn require leadership. Several of the gardens in this study were started by libraries with a staff person determined to create a garden. In these cases, one person can provide the push to start a garden, even without a community organization to assist. Those started by only one person may attract the attention of other garden lovers, and those interested in community beautification.

These are photos of the Imaginarium Garden at the Southfield Public Library in Michigan. The garden is a walled-in oasis from the busy library and features a butterfly bench, outdoor story circle, and a ten-foot-tall sculpture, at the top of which is a facsimile of Frances Hodgson Burnett's classic book *The Secret Garden* which acts as a weather vane. Alice's Adventures in Wonderland has a prism for the light to shine through, and you can climb on top of the Very Hungry Caterpillar. The garden also has artwork, including a tile series, *Season of the Imagination,* by local artist Laurie Eisenhardt; Wooden Birdhouses by Naturally Wood; and two sculptures by the Gary Lee Price Studios: *Journey of the Imagination* and *Words of Wisdom Girl.*

Imaginarium Garden, Southfield Public Library, Southfield, Michigan. Photos courtesy Don Meadow.

Library gardens come in a variety of sizes, with no established pattern or preference for a particular size. Generally, they seem to grow to fit an available space. The largest garden in this survey, at the Mid Columbia Library in Washington, was three acres; many smaller library gardens, including planter gardens, and every size in between were represented.

For a library to have a garden it is not necessary to start with a large piece of land. Gardens are placed where it is convenient to have a space of land transformed, or in an area bordered by sidewalks or curbs. Many gardens have not changed in size during their tenure at the library, while others expand with the interest shown by communities. The Salem, Wisconsin, garden started out as a small planting around a water feature, but grew into a large plot highlighting the library. The University City Public Library has gardens on all four sides of the building, while other libraries have small gardens or oddly shaped gardens that will fit into a small, otherwise unused piece of land in the midst of crisscrossing sidewalks.

Library gardens across the country grow a wide variety of different plants, depending on the desires and availability for the garden project. Many libraries grow flowers, which are enjoyed by staff and the community alike. Some, like the Salt Lake City library, grow trees and special grasses. The Kenosha Public Library in Wisconsin grows ornamental grasses and flowers, but also maintains a topiary in the middle of the garden. It is cut into the shape of a bookworm, which they have named Dewey, which is covered with ivy, has reading glasses made of copper, and is reading a book made of cement. The Pulaski County Public Library in Somerset, Kentucky, has a horticultural garden with many different features, including topiaries, vermicomposting, bird and bat habitats, and a water feature. Additionally, it functions as an outdoor classroom. The University City Public Library grows a variety of vegetables, including tomatoes, cucumbers, and squash. They also have an apple tree, an assortment of perennials, a herb garden, and a butterfly garden.

Libraries that embrace the idea of gardening may then expand their plans for multiple gardens. The Mid Columbia Library in Washington maintains a variety of different demonstration gardens. They include a butterfly garden, herb garden, and Japanese garden. In addition, they have a vegetable garden, which grows food to be donated to a local food bank. They also have a composting demonstration area, a formal garden, and a Jackson and Perkins test garden for new rose varieties, and they use xeriscaping to promote water conservation. These gardens serve to not only provide benefits to the library but also help community organizations have a venue to work with the public.

Other gardens are designed to showcase one particular system of gardening, for educational purposes. The Whitestone Community Library, Queens Library has a garden designed for reading and contemplation. It has decorative plants and trees for people to enjoy while they are in the garden. Some gardens, such as the Addison Public Library in Illinois, focus on native plants for their area, or on providing drought-tolerant plants. The Sam J. Racadio Library & Environmental Learning Center garden not only has native plants in its garden, but also maintains a composting area and a turtle habitat and pond as part of the garden area.

Issues in the gardens: problems and solutions

Gardens are not without their problems, and those on library grounds are no exception. Many libraries mentioned the continuing issues they have with garden maintenance. As one respondent summed up their gardening issues: "weeds, weeds, weeds." Specific issues with individual gardens were noted by several libraries. The work of changing the soil and plants in the garden is exacerbated with a rooftop garden. The Zion-Benton Public Library has a more common problem: continuing access to water is difficult, as the hose spigot is on the opposite side of the building from the garden, pointing to the need for a whole-facility approach to garden planning.

Being able to start projects for little or no money is particularly important for libraries in these times of shrinking budgets, so donations and financial assistance from their Friends organizations were essential for many libraries. "Originally we thought it would take a lot of money to buy plants, but we teamed up with two local organizations who ended up donating all the plants and seedlings," reported the Grand Rapids Public Library. The Mahopac Public Library in New York adds, "The community—the Garden Club, a donor, and a local landscaper—stepped up to the plate in terms of funding the plantings. We also have engraved pavers in the gardens—another fund-raiser," while the Akron Public Library agreed: "Everything in the garden was paid for with grants and donations; no money was taken from the library budget."

Nonetheless, administrators were encouraged to be mindful of the potential costs involved in a garden. "Determine the primary purpose of the garden, location, initial cost, ongoing cost, location, and design," suggested the Addison Public Library. "Research carefully, talk to libraries that have initiated some kind of garden, and plan for its use."

A key finding relates to the value of gardens in enriching the experience of place. "It makes a very attractive, welcoming addition to the library. Patrons can wait in there until we open. It is covered by a ceiling of trellising, to ease the sun during the summer," reports the South Coastal Library in Bethany Beach, Delaware. The Newport Beach Public Library added, "The City Council and the community in general embraced the project, and it brought in some great publicity. It provides a place for restless kids to go and release some noise." The Salt Lake City library said one of the benefits of their garden is that it "lends beauty to the roof and it creates a relaxing atmosphere for our staff and patrons." The Downtown Reno branch, Washoe County Library commented that their garden "makes for a very attractive, unique, and beloved space." "Whatever you do, people will respond because people want a quiet space and to enjoy nature," adds the Poplar Creek Public Library District. This theme also resonated with the Howe Library in Hanover, New Hampshire: "It's a treat to see a family eating their lunch out there, seeing someone Skype with a friend in Germany, seeing the teens eating popsicles on hot days, and more."

Other library gardeners commented that the garden, in addition to providing another place for the public to gather and enjoy visiting while at the library, is a resource for teaching the community about green resources and gardening ideas.

"We have been able to educate thousands of patrons on composting and native plants," said the Sam J. Racadio Library & Environmental Learning Center.

The experienced libraries had a lot of advice to pass on to libraries that may be considering starting a garden of their own. Librarians were uniformly enthusiastic about the benefits a garden can provide to a library and the community it serves, despite challenges that need to be addressed. The Salt Lake City library suggested rethinking a rooftop garden to prevent the risk of leaks.

Discussion

Public libraries with gardens are demonstrating at least two important aspects of resiliency: self-organization, and flexibility/adaptability. These are truly examples of people coming together to innovate new ways of networking and exchanging information. Many of these gardens were started by one individual with an interest in the subject, who then created a network of people within the library and in the community to help see the vision through to reality. These gardens are also examples of the flexibility shown in public libraries: rather than being rigidly tied to information sharing only in a traditional way, or only through certain transmission channels (such as the book, or the computer), libraries with gardens are transmitting information in a more dynamic, physical way. Libraries are showing the value gardens can bring to a building and to a community; by providing community members the opportunity to work in the garden, or to learn more about gardening, they are both providing a significant community space and are helping connect urban residents to nature.

Libraries considering gardens have a wide array of choices to make in the development of their own garden to make it the best possible fit for their community. Gardens can be very fancy and intricate and expensive, or they can be quite small and housed inside the building. They can be driven by one gardener on staff, or can be created by community members. Gardens may be included in the construction plans of a new building, or may be located in some previously unused part of the library.

After reviewing all the information on developing and maintaining a library garden from the libraries around the country that already maintain gardens, several guidelines emerge:

- Make connections in the community to other potential gardeners who may help you. But do not be discouraged if you have to start a small garden on your own.

- When putting together plans for the garden, find more people to participate than you may really need; some of them will not be able to follow through with helping.

- Remember the financial cost of a garden, and factor that ongoing expense into your plans. Before the start-up, work with partners from across the community to help with beginning funds for plants, equipment, and any necessary pre-gardening work that may need to be done.

- When planning a new building, consider putting in a new garden! The extra effort needed when starting up a garden can be taken care of at that time, making it even easier to get your garden up and running.

One area that all the responding libraries lacked was a marketing presence built around their garden. Very few had any photos available online about the garden, or any report about the garden and the successes they have had with it. A garden can be a natural part of a marketing plan, and adding photos to the library's website and to Flickr and other social media sites may help to draw the attention of people who may not otherwise be attracted to the library.

Gardens are not the only way to connect a public library with nature. The Evanston Public Library, outside Chicago, does not have a garden, but they do have a pair of peregrine falcons (Nona and Squawker) nesting at the library every year. The library maintains an active Facebook page for falcon news, a section on their website with an archive of pictures of the eggs, parents, and babies from each year, and also contributes to an electronic discussion list set up by fans of the falcons. With the strong support of community falcon lovers, they upgraded the still camera they were using to take periodic photos of the falcon activities to a live video camera. This allows falcon fans around the country to watch the falcons as they lay eggs, and to watch the babies hatch and grow up to leave the nest. The library also participates in the annual banding of the babies—which happens inside the library, with the video available on the library website. This brings in not only library users, but also others who may not think of the public library as an environmental participant in the community—who may stay to use library resources! This type of social media connection between the library and an environmental practice could be a model libraries could adapt to fit the needs of their library gardens, sharing photos and information on the positive environmental benefits for their communities.

Based on the experiences and feedback received from libraries across the country, it is clear that a library garden is a positive service and a way to enhance public spaces and benefit the community. When so many city-dwellers—especially those removed from access to riverfronts or forests—have limited contact with green and growing things, a library garden can meet an important and ingrained human need for contact with nature. Even working with indoor gardens throughout the library—flower pots, plants, and so on—when an outdoor garden is not possible, will bring benefits. It should help to lift the spirits of staff, patrons, and community members alike. Furthermore, the benefits of working with members of the community on gardening projects are numerous. Helping people learn firsthand about good environmental practices is a great way of developing closer ties between the library and patrons, which can encourage them to return for other programs, materials, and services. Library gardens can contribute to community cohesion and hence resiliency by building relationships between the library, local businesses, schools, and organizations.

Resources for more information on library gardens

American Community Gardening Association: www.communitygarden.org.

Burek Pierce, Jennifer. "Blooming Booklovers." *American Libraries* 38, no. 3 (March 2007): 79.

———. "One of the 'World's Most Beautiful Libraries.'" *American Libraries* 35, no. 5 (May 2004): 55.

Eubank, Susan. "Volunteers in the Helen Fowler Library at Denver Botanic Gardens." *Colorado Libraries* 25, no. 3 (Fall 1999): 51.

Hustedde, Hedy N. R. "Emily Dickinson Lives! @ the Bettendorf Public Library." *Public Libraries* 44, no. 5 (September/October 2005): 287–91.

Kuzyk, Raya. "Learning Gardens." *Library Journal* 132, no. 17 (October 2007): 40–43.

Thorner, J. Lincoln. "On Assignment: Brooklyn Botanic Garden Library." *Wilson Library Bulletin* 62 (February 1988): 57–59.

NOTES

1. Jolanda Maas and others, "Green Space, Urbanity, and Health: How Strong Is the Relation?" *Journal of Epidemiological Community Health* 60, no. 7 (2006): 587–92.

2. For an extensive selection of research papers on themes related to the psychosocial benefits of nature on communities and in urban settings, see the work of Dr. Frances E. Kuo at the Landscape and Human Health Laboratory at the University of Illinois at Urbana-Champaign: http://lhhl.illinois.edu/all.scientific.articles.htm.

3. Richard Louv, *Last Child in the Woods: Saving Our Children from Nature-Deficit Disorder* (Chapel Hill, NC: Thomas Allen, 2005).

Partners for the future
Public libraries and local governments creating sustainable communities

Local governments are leading the way in confronting the connected economic, environmental, and social equity challenges that are essential to the long-term health and vitality of North America's counties, cities, and towns. Public libraries are emerging as strategic partners with their local governments in shaping and achieving sustainability goals. Libraries' solid community connections, stature as highly trusted public institutions, capacity to deliver programs and distribute information to large and diverse audiences, and universal accessibility make them logical partners in what the International City/County Management Association called sustainability "the issue of our age."[1]

Local governments are broadening and deepening their commitment to sustainability. There is an increased awareness of the linkages among economic, environmental, and social equity challenges and how local governments must make decisions today with an eye toward the future. While many local sustainability plans began with a commitment to environmental preservation, the triple bottom line is now the driving framework, with economic prosperity generally leading the way. Actions local governments are taking to address the triple bottom line include developing comprehensive plans; creating community advisory groups to engage and inform the public; viewing sustainability as a philosophy and a decision-making process more than as a government "program"; hiring full-time sustainability officers to coordinate actions; leveraging federal funds to support sustainability strategies; and signing onto national sustainability commitments designed to raise awareness and produce collective results. For example, more than 1,000 United States mayors have signed the Mayors' Climate Protection agreement in which they commit to reducing emissions in their cities to 7 percent below the 1990 levels by 2012.

Public libraries' direct engagement in local government sustainability plans vary considerably. Many library programs support local sustainability priorities whether or not the library is an active player at the local government table. Literacy programs, job skills and job-seeking services, universal Internet access, environmental information, and model green practices, all provided by the library, contribute to community sustainability. When the public library is a local government department, involvement in sustainability priorities is obviously the strongest. However, regardless of the structural relationship, connecting public library programs and capacities to local government priorities will enhance results. Not making the connection, many local officials say, is a missed opportunity.

Because local governments and libraries serve the same constituency, ensuring close program connections advances local agendas. Constituents think of their library as a reliable and trusted public resource. When a public library is named for the city or county in which it is located, residents assume it is a local government service. So, in cities and counties where the library is a separate organization, leveraging the identity connection to become a strategic program connection makes good political sense. Local governments have maximized those connections by using library facilities for vital public meetings, drawing on library communication and outreach capacities to connect with shared constituencies, and depending on libraries to deliver essential services that support local priorities. "In any county, the public library is a major part of the community infrastructure," says Jay Fisette, chairman of the Arlington, Virginia, County Board. "People in the county identify with it."

Successful partnerships emerge from active outreach. Structure does not determine how partnerships work—people do. In many cases, the library director must take the first step. Cleveland's Chief of Sustainability Andrew Watterson says, "I didn't think of the library as a natural home for a sustainability resource center until Felton (Felton Thomas, Jr., director of the Cleveland Public Library) came and presented his plan. After the presentation, we all looked at each other and said, 'Of course this is a good place.'" As a result of that outreach, the city and the public library have worked together to build the resource center to support Sustainable Cleveland 2019, the mayor's long-term action plan. Nashville Public Library Director Donna Nicely says she regularly takes the first step to ensure that library programs support the mayor's priorities. For example, to support Mayor Karl Dean's interest in increased use of rapid bus transportation, Nicely made locating library branches along bus routes a priority. "Libraries should consider locations based on public transportation because it makes the library more accessible to everyone and reduces the need to drive," Nicely says.

Local governments and libraries can be powerful partners in building sustainable communities. They are cut from the same public service cloth and share the same values and commitment to building strong, healthy, engaged, resilient, and sustainable communities. By working together, local governments and libraries enhance resources dedicated to achieving sustainability goals, leverage the libraries' expertise to support local priorities, and strengthen connections to their shared constituencies. Libraries have also brought corporate partners to the table. Corporations such as Aflac, the supplemental insurance provider in Columbus, Georgia, and Covidien, the health products and services provider in New Haven, Connecticut, have helped strengthen their contributions to achieving sustainability goals.

Library governance and local government partnerships

Governance relationships between local governments and public libraries vary widely. But library and local government leaders agree that governance is, but should not be, an obstacle to effective partnerships. A recent Urban Libraries Council survey highlighted the diversity of library structures. Of the responding libraries, 32 percent were city or county departments, 19 percent were independent agencies of a city or county government with a board appointed by the city or county government, 16 percent were special taxing districts, 11 percent were nonprofit organizations, and 3 percent were part of the school district. Another 19 percent reported other structures, including joint city-county agency, independent agency with both state funding and special taxing capacity, semi-independent agency, joint powers authority, and political subdivision of the state.[2] City Manager Rashad Young of Greensboro, North Carolina, learned the value of having the library director among his department heads after working in two cities where the public libraries were independent agencies. "This is a department I didn't have in my previous jobs. The library was there, but not part of my daily focus," Young says. "In Greensboro, I have become acutely aware of what the library means to the community—and how it contributes to improving the quality of life here. I regularly look to the library on a variety of programs, particularly around small business services and job connectivity/job searching for local residents." In Fayetteville, Arkansas, the public library is an independent agency governed by a board of trustees appointed by the mayor, with 51 percent of its operating budget coming from the city. Nevertheless, the library's position as a core service in Fayetteville evolved from sustained working relationships around local priorities and a willingness to take on new challenges. "The thing the library has been successful with is to say what are the goals of city government, what are the goals of the mayor, and this is what we can do to help you accomplish that goal," Fayetteville Chief of Staff Don Marr says.

In University Place, Washington, a new branch of the Pierce County Library is a key component of a town center development plan. The library system is governed by a five-member board of trustees appointed by the Pierce County executive with no direct connection to University Place—except that one of its seventeen branches, the University Place Public Library, is located within the city limits. The city and the library system entered into an agreement to build the new library as one of the anchors for the town center, in part because of its ability to draw people. "Electrons start buzzing around the library," says Interim City Manager Steve Suggs. "People connect to the library as a valuable and safe place—a resource that is not going away." "We're joined at the hip because the library and city hall are the anchors of our new town center," Suggs says. "But it is deeper than that. Citizens see the library as a city function, so it is important that I operate that way. And we benefit in many ways from their presence in the center of our downtown."

When local governments and public libraries are joined at the hip around sustainability goals, residents are more likely to be active, engaged, and informed and the opportunities for achieving results enhanced.

Sustainability has its roots in environmental preservation. For many local governments, the commitment to establish green goals was designed to preserve and protect the environment, which in turn broadened the sustainability focus. Local environmental sustainability goals are built around reducing energy consumption to meet defined targets, employing green land use planning and building practices, and engaging the community in environmental sustainability efforts. Public libraries support environmental sustainability goals by

- modeling green practices in building and operations;
- serving as test centers for energy conservation innovation;
- engaging the community in supporting local environmental goals; and
- educating the public about environmental sustainability in general and local priorities in particular.

The following sections provide examples of how public libraries and local governments are working together to achieve environmental sustainability goals.

Modeling green practices

Public libraries have embraced green building and green operations, working in close partnership with local governments. As more and more governments adopt green building policies and requirements, new public libraries have become models of creative design and measurable energy savings. Green roofs, solar panels, geothermal heating systems, on-demand water heating, glazed windows, skylights, and use of recycled materials throughout buildings are becoming the norm in today's modern libraries. Library staff involvement through environmental committees, green teams, and individual leadership focus on green operations and connect library operations to local government energy-saving practices. What makes green building and operations in public libraries particularly valuable is their educational impact. Every visit to a green public library is a lesson learned about environmental construction and energy-efficient operations. Tours of green roofs, kiosks telling the library's green story, demonstrations of how solar panels on library buildings generate energy, and visible recycling activities raise awareness about the importance of collective community action to preserve environmental resources.

Test centers for energy conservation innovation

The Fayetteville Public Library and the city of Fayetteville are working together to bring solar energy to market in the region. The library is considered the city's laboratory. With a grant from the International City/County Management Association (ICMA), the Fayetteville team designed and installed sixty solar panels on the library's roof to provide power to the library using a commercially available inverter. As part of the research process, the library tested a highly efficient, state-of-the-art silicon converter developed by Arkansas Power Electronics International, a small local company that specializes in developing technology for electronic systems. The project has broad sustainability goals beyond improving energy efficiency, including

- strengthening and broadening community partnerships around environmental sustainability goals with the library as the linchpin;
- contributing to a regional goal of developing a "green valley" in northwest Arkansas by providing opportunities for local companies to develop and run new solar energy technologies and putting the library at the center of these efforts; and
- educating the public about alternative energy sources and motivating them to consider trying new approaches to reduce their energy consumption.

"The city of Fayetteville is on the cutting edge of exposing the broad role that public libraries can play in responding to community priorities," says Ron Carlee, ICMA chief operating officer and director of strategic initiatives. "Their solar test bed project is clearly non-traditional for a library, but is important to their community."[3]

Engaging the public in supporting local environmental goals

Many libraries have created comprehensive outreach programs designed to broaden awareness of environmental sustainability issues. Because of the diverse audiences they serve and their position as a trusted resource, libraries effectively connect the public to environmental sustainability challenges and opportunities.

For example, the Arlington Public Library in Virginia hosted a speakers' series featuring prominent authors who addressed specific aspects of the county's environmental sustainability agenda. With the county board chair in attendance, the standing room-only sessions increased knowledge about sustainability and connected residents to the local government's sustainability strategy.

The San Francisco Public Library's "Green Stacks" is designed to increase awareness of environmental sustainability, connect residents to local priorities, and extend the local government's reach into underserved communities. The program provides a one-stop environmental sustainability action center—green building, green practices, green programming, green bibliography, and a community awareness and marketing program about everything green, working in partnership with the local government environment office.

Library officials are focusing particularly on ensuring that the program reaches residents in poor and underserved communities to give them access to information about healthy and sustainable lifestyle choices. Green Stacks components include compostable plastic library cards, an interactive display that teaches eco-literacy to young children, a comprehensive website, community gardens and green roofs at two branch libraries, and comprehensive educational programs for children, teens, and adults.

Educating the public about environmental responsibility

In addition to modeling, public libraries help achieve environmental sustainability goals by educating the public about environmental awareness, responsibility, and action. Library roles in environmental sustainability education are broad, deep, ongoing, and valued. Expert speakers, special environmental sections of library websites, demonstrations of ways to build green homes, workshops on topics such as greening your life, special youth programs to introduce kids to green activities, access to tools that measure electric consumption and appliance efficiency, and even a dedicated environmental library have drawn high interest.

Environmental library

The Greensboro Public Library has a branch that is devoted to environmental education and action, working closely with organizations through the region that are committed to environmental sustainability. The Kathleen Clay Edwards Family Branch is located in a 98-acre park that provides extensive nature, gardening, and environmental resources for children and adults. According to Environmental Resources Librarian Melanie Buckingham, the library has become a model for environmental practice, a well-known resource throughout the state for environmental education, and a community hub for environmental information, education, and action. In addition to workshops, publications, and videos, the library offers hands-on programs on gardening, conservation, "eco-teering" through field trips and hikes, and kids' nature days that draw on the surrounding park.

Connecting literacy and environmental awareness

Jacksonville, Florida, Mayor John Peyton has connected his personal commitment to early literacy with environmental education for toddlers. The Mayor's

Book Club, whose target audience is prekindergarten kids, includes a "great outdoors adventure" component that focuses on conservation and the environment, encouraging members and their families to enjoy the city's natural assets. The program includes monthly activities, educational programming at local parks, and story times hosted through a partnership between the Jacksonville Public Library and the Parks Department. The program has added green practices to model what they are teaching, including providing a reusable tote bag for program materials, printing all materials locally on recycled paper, giving everyone a new book called *We're Going Green,* and encouraging paperless online registration.[4]

"Being a reliable resource on green issues is an important way to position the library as bringing value to the community and supporting environmental sustainability goals," says Multnomah County Director of Libraries Vailey Oehlke. "Our educational programs about environmental sustainability convey to the community that we make a real difference in the quality of life."

Emerging opportunities

Local governments and libraries can strengthen environmental sustainability outcomes by the following:

Utilizing libraries as learning labs. Fayetteville Chief of Staff Don Marr sees the public library as the city's personal learning lab. Its solar test bed project, according to Marr, is only one example of how the library provides research capacity to support sustainability goals. "Working together, we can incubate new patented ideas and business partners while achieving incremental change in our energy efficiency rating," Marr says.[5] Being a successful learning lab requires a willingness on the part of libraries to take on new challenges to help advance local agendas.

Connecting library resources to sustainability goals. Books, workshops, and videos that educate the public about environmental sustainability are useful. Resources that inform residents about local goals and provide tools to engage residents in achieving those goals are even more valuable. The Cleveland Public Library created a sustainability resource center that supports the mayor's long-term goals. Working in partnership with the mayor's sustainability office, the library has organized resources around targets in the plan, including information about sustainability in general, green jobs, energy efficiency, new green technology, recycling, and more, with knowledgeable library staff nearby to provide direct assistance.

Including library staff as resources to community task forces. Inviting library staff to participate in community task force meetings as observers, listeners, staff resources, or members will ensure that the library is aware of community directions and needs. That awareness will help the library connect its programs to local government priorities and community interests.

The findings that emerged from in-depth interviews with local officials and library directors point to both powerful existing partnerships and opportunities for deeper connections to achieve lasting results for sustainable communities.

NOTES

1. "Sustainability," ICMA Management Perspective, International City/County Management Association, October 2007.

2. The data was collected by Community Research Partners for the Urban Libraries Council, August 2009.

3. "A Library Spurs Economic Development," International City/County Management Association, Washington, DC, July 22, 2010, icma.org/en/Article/100460/ A_Library_Spurs_ Economic_Development.

4. "The State of City Leadership for Children and Families," National League of Cities, Institute for Youth, Education, and Families, Washington, DC, 2009, p. 9.

5. This is part of a joint city-public library-university partnership to test solar technology as an alternative energy source; see *Partners for the Future*, p. 16.

Adapted with permission from chapters 1 and 3 of the Urban Libraries Council's report "Partners for the Future: Public Libraries and Local Governments Creating Sustainable Communities" (2010). For the full report, see www.libraryworks.com/INFOcus/1210/ ULC_Sustainable_Communities_Full_Report.pdf.

chapter ten

Maija Berndtson

A "people's palace"
Public libraries and placemaking

The city of Birmingham's (UK) new library will be located very centrally in Centenary Square, the city's largest public square and next to Birmingham Symphony Hall. Together with the theater, the new library will bring the spoken and written word together and will focus on learning, access, and digitization and will provide a social heart for Birmingham, a city with one of the youngest and most diverse populations in Europe.

When completed in mid-2013, the new building will be in stark contrast to the existing central library from 1974, which is a typical example of the brutal concrete architecture of the era. Francine Houben, the Dutch architect whose firm Mecanoo Architecten was chosen to design Birmingham's new library, stated in 2008 that "we hope to create a people's palace, warm and welcoming."[1]

Like other cities' new library projects, Birmingham's demonstrates the evolution of the public library: they are no longer just places of reading and private study, but are community and cultural centers, living rooms for cities, digital hubs and mediatheques, and are not just for the storage and access of print.[2] The library is a "people's palace" and a key element in urban placemaking.

A renaissance of libraries in urban planning

There seems to be a boom of new library buildings in European cities and not only in capitals, but also in smaller cities. Since 2003 new central libraries have

Rendering of the new Library of Birmingham, United Kingdom, opening June 2013. Image courtesy Birmingham Library and Archive Service.

been opened in Vienna in 2003; Amsterdam in 2007; Drammen, Norway, in 2007; Helsingör, Denmark, in 2010; Turku, Finland, in 2007; and Newcastle-upon-Tyne in 2009, just to name a few.

In recent years there have been high-profile architectural competitions for new libraries in Århus (Denmark), Oslo, Barcelona, Stuttgart, Stockholm, and Birmingham. Stuttgart's new public library opened in October 2011, while Birmingham's is scheduled for 2013. Helsinki's Public Library meanwhile has launched a major architectural competition for its Central Library and, with over 500 entries received to date, hopes to have narrowed this to a field of 6 to 8 by September 2012.[3] Key to this competition is the newly refined vision of the Helsinki Public Library as "an enricher of ideas and thoughts, whereby sharing knowledge, skills and stories we create together a new civic society."[4]

A common denominator for all these projects is that they are very much connected to the development of city centers and to the urban planning process in general. The local circumstances can vary, from having empty areas in city centers, remodeling old industrial and harbor areas (Århus, Helsingör, Amsterdam), or creating new cultural areas (Oslo).

Even if all these libraries have had very well-formulated reasons for developing a new building, the real start has mainly happened when the project has become a part of a bigger city development project. But why is this so? The answer is perhaps connected to the ideas underlying the research project "Public Libraries in Urban Development—Creativity, Innovation and Experience" at the Centre for Cultural

Rendering of Urban Mediaspace Århus, Denmark, Image courtesy of Schmidt Hammer Lassen Architects.

Policy Studies at the Royal Danish School of Library and Information Science from 2010–11.[5] The research explores the following questions:

- What is the role of the library in these models and strategies for urban and cultural planning?
- What is the role of public libraries in different strategies of culture-led re-generation?
- How do these tendencies challenge the design, the concept, and the mission of the public library?

The starting point of this project is that cities everywhere are competing globally and need new approaches and ideas. Libraries can be a part of the solution, but can't simply repeat the same models everywhere. The researchers ask that librarians consider what the library can do for society and not the opposite. The study finds that, with their often iconic architecture, public library projects—as a part of the "cultural turn" in cities—are major forces in placemaking.[6] In their later research, however, the project's researchers query why there are, on the global level, so few iconic library buildings compared with art museums and concert halls. Have library administrators been too conventional and merely followed the mainstream? My answer to this question would be that public libraries have not belonged or catered to the cultural elite, suggesting that—after the Carnegie library building program, at least—only occasionally were marvelous buildings built to house libraries. Now, however, iconic buildings include existing libraries such as the Biblioteca Alexandria and the Seattle Public Library, and the new libraries in Birmingham, Oslo, and Århus.

While the number of iconic library buildings can be counted on the fingers of one hand, the Public Libraries in Urban Development researchers see more successful examples of libraries as placemakers that are used to strengthen city centers or to revitalize earlier industrial or harbor areas. Libraries can also be catalysts for local development, like "Idea Store" libraries in the London borough of Tower Hamlets (UK).

Just as cities work to develop open, living, and multifunctional spaces, the same design trends are apparent in the layout and interior of libraries. The rational reading room is replaced by more inspiring spaces that offer possibilities for meetings and experiences. Many of the new library buildings extend the public domain area of the city, which makes public libraries places where people meet other people with different backgrounds, ages, and lifestyles, and from various social groups.

These examples and more demonstrate that public libraries are increasingly being seen as a strategic factor in the development of attractive, living, and multiform cities. These aspects of city building are reflected in the architectural expression, design, and functions of library buildings.

For an American librarian this proposed new attitude and the questions raised by the Public Libraries in Urban Development study might not seem all that surprising or even anything new. I personally feel that libraries in the United States have always been working toward being a strong part of society and attentive to its needs. But in Nordic countries and even in other countries in Europe this is—if not exactly revolutionary—at least a little bit surprising. On the other hand, there already exists at least one example which shows that this could be the right direction. I refer here to London's Idea Stores.[7]

London does not have any central library or a common library system, but local governments are free to develop their own libraries. The starting point for the change was that in the London borough of Tower Hamlets library use rates were extremely low, and the borough wanted to do something to alter this. Customer surveys revealed that people would like shopping and banking during the same visit and that they wanted to do many other things besides borrowing books when at the library.

The result was that the old libraries (some of them Carnegie buildings) were closed and new libraries were situated closer to the shopping areas. A new, colorful library concept was created, and even the name of library was changed to the Idea Store. The explanation for the change of name was that in these immigrant-dominated areas, people came from countries where they did not have any experience with what a public library is and what it could offer. But the Idea Store planners also wanted to get rid of the image of the earlier libraries. The renewal has been widely considered a success, as the use of Idea Stores has increased enormously and now the concept will be implemented in other boroughs, too. I do not know how well-known Idea Stores are in the United States, but the transformation the Danish researchers are recommending has already more or less happened in these libraries.

A public space that enables and empowers

When we consider public libraries, one remarkable aspect is that they are one of the few public places and spaces left in most cities. Public spaces are those that are open and accessible to all, regardless of gender, race, ethnicity, age, or socio-economic level, such as town squares and parks. However, traditions related to "the commons" have suffered with increased privatization: for example, shopping malls with the appearance of being a "public space"—but are actually *privately owned public spaces.* The concept of "public" is so important, writes Columbia University urban theorist Rosalyn Deutsche, because the term

> has democratic connotations. It implies "openness," "accessibility," "participation," "inclusion," and "accountability." . . . "Public space" in this view does not simply refer to already existing, physical urban sites such as parks, urban squares, streets, or cities as a whole. Of course, parks, squares, and other elements of the built environment can be public spaces. But they are not self-evidently public, nor are they the only public spaces. The concept of the public sphere makes it clear that public space cannot be reduced to empirically identifiable spaces. Public space can also be defined as a set of institutions where citizens—and, given the unprecedented mixing of foreigners in today's international cities, hopefully non-citizens—engage in debate; as the space where rights are declared, thereby limiting power; or as the space where social group identities and the identity of society are both constituted and questioned.[8]

The institution of the public library is clearly relevant here. The picture of public space becomes still more active and easier to understand when we consider Ray Oldenburg and his ideas about "the third place" (apart from home and work) or "the great good place."[9] Oldenburg identifies third places as the public places on neutral ground where people can gather and interact. He characterizes the third place as follows:

- a neutral ground upon which people may gather
- a leveler, an inclusive place, that does not set formal criteria for membership and exclusion
- conversation is the main activity
- accessibility and accommodation; it keeps long hours
- the regulars, that is, people who come regularly
- a low profile; it is easy to come to, and the threshold is low
- the mood is playful
- a home away from home, as cozy as home

Oldenburg also says that third places appear to be universal and essential to a vital informal public life. But when he counts cafés, coffee shops, bookstores, bars, hair salons, and other hangouts at the heart of a community as third places he makes a mistake; he does not mention public libraries! On the other hand, I have just recently come to understood why Oldenburg very likely did not include libraries in his examination of third places. He wrote his books over twenty years ago; if we think how libraries looked and functioned at that time, they lacked many of the required characteristics of a third place. For me understanding this fact gives hope and new impetus: in twenty years libraries have changed!

The public library "takes place"—but is it still a library?

The Swedish historian Rasmus Fleischer says that "the culture takes place."[10] In the heading for this section, I quote Fleischer but replace the word *culture* with *public library*. His expression is intentionally ambiguous, but the basic message is that, whether we are talking about cultural output or public libraries, we have to defend their right to "take our place" in the society. In a world where the digital part of our lives is increasing, we have to understand that the reality of the twenty-first century will be a combination of the physical and digital. On the other hand, the digital influences the physical. Before the Internet every branch library in its isolation had to be a small universe with books about "everything," but the situation is totally different today. The number of physical objects in the library premises, both smaller and bigger, can be more limited when we can use material which is in databases or exists in e-format.

It is a paradoxical reality that the more digital material we have outside the library, the more important the physical library and its interior become. In the future, the library will not be mainly for the storage of books but a place for people to connect and collaborate in a "third place"—libraries will really become meeting places of people and ideas. In this case we have to give more and different types of space to people who come to the library to do different things.

At the same time there is also the question of the extent to which the library will actually be used as a meeting place when so many other places—with comfortable seating, food, and free wireless—also want to be regarded as living rooms and meeting places. If, however, we combine the task of the public library—to support democracy, culture, and development through people—with the concept of meeting rooms and the idea of public space, then the importance of the role of public libraries is very clear.

In this chapter I have referred only to big library building projects. But cities need all kinds of public libraries, including small ones. Libraries have to be close to people and easy to reach, so they have to be in places where people are living, working, and meeting their daily needs.

As libraries move toward these other ideas in terms of public space and different kinds of activities—instead of merely storing books—it means that we also will have many more different actors and partners in our premises. This leads me to a question that is painful but which I have to raise, namely: should public libraries be called libraries in the future? In Tower Hamlets they have already changed the name. And in Italy I have had very intensive discussions about this topic. Some Italian librarians think that in their country the concept of "library" is so much connected with books that they will never be able to change the image and activities of the library to reflect digital realities using that name. In Århus the name of the new library building is Mediaspace.

I recognize the same trend in the United States, too, when I read in *Library Journal* about the Adams County Library System and its Rangeview Library, which was transformed into Anythink.[11] The change (which was presented in 2010 at the annual conference of the Public Library Association) is framed as revolutionary: even the new brand and logo emphasize this aspect, saying "Anythink—A Revolution of Rangeview Libraries." The revolution is described with three points: dropping Dewey decimals for an intuitive "WordThink" term-based system, new jobs ("wranglers," "concierge," and "guides"), and new buildings aimed at replicating a more casual, bookstore experience while being fun and ecologically sustainable. The changes have been very enthusiastically received.

The interesting thing about the new names like Idea Stores and Anythink is that they emphasize the user and the reactions in the user's mind and his or her behavior. The leading role has been moved from the institution to the individual, which is totally correct since the impact of library activities can be reached only through people who use the library.

The concept of the "library" has a long tradition and a storied reputation. In a country like Finland people love their libraries as traditionally conceived and they would likely be totally confused if we were to change the name of the library. Many people connect the idea of library very much to borrowing and to printed books, and sometimes people want to have the traditional library—even if they would not use it more. Our challenge as librarians is how to renew our libraries. The name *library* is not necessarily an obstacle to digital and service innovation, as we in the Helsinki City Library have proved. Our newest and one of the most popular libraries, Library 10, is the most customer-driven and radical in our system. It is in transformation all the time, according to the wishes of its users, and 80 percent of the programming on the stage of the library is organized and performed by the customers. Library 10 is, on a small scale, a people's palace.

The question facing public libraries now is, how much can we change the library in a digital age without changing its relationship to place? Will we lose something in the transition from public library to "people's palace"? In my mind whatever new model emerges and whatever names they will have, these "library-like" people's palaces have to reflect the dynamic and innovative role libraries have always had in peoples' lives, within cities, and on society.

NOTES

1. "Mecanoo Wins £193m Library of Birmingham Competition," *Bustler,* August 5, 2008, www.bustler.net/index.php/article/mecanoo_wins_193m_library_of_birmingham_competition/.

2. Francine Houben, "Library of the 21st Century," London Festival of Architecture, June 20, 2010, www.lfa2010.org/event.php?id=267&name=francine_houben_library_of_the_21st_century.

3. "The Heart of the Metropolis: Helsinki Central Library Open Architectural Competition," http://cpmpetition.keskustakirjasto.fi.

4. Helsinki City Library, www.lib.hel.fi/en-GB/organisaatio/.

5. Henrik Jochumsen, Casper Hvenegaard Rasmussen, and Dorte Skot-Hansen, "Biblioteket som strategisk faktor i byudvikling," *Danmarks Biblioteker* no. 4

(2011), http://pure.iva.dk/en/publications/biblioteket-som-strategisk-faktor -i-byudvikling(442913d7-0123-429f-a9d4-bccc511ca30c).html.

6. In South Africa, the same has been applied to some extent with notable success (Theron and Maphunye, 2005; Greyling, 2007).

7. "Libraries and Learning in Tower Hamlets," *The Idea Store,* www.ideastore.co.uk/.

8. Rosalyn Deutsche, "The Question of Public Space," American Photography Institute, National Graduate Seminar, June 1–13, 1998, www.thephotography institute.org/journals/1998/rosalyn_deutsche.html.

9. Ray Oldenburg, *The Great Good Place: Cafes, Coffee Shops, Bookstores, Bars, Hair Salons, and Other Hangouts at the Heart of a Community* (New York: Marlowe, 1989).

10. "Rasmus Fleischer," *Wikipedia,* http://en.wikipedia.org/wiki/Rasmus_Fleischer. The essay being cited in this chapter ("Det Postdigitala Manifestet") is not available in English.

11. Norman Older, "The Anythink Revolution Is Ripe," *Library Journal,* March 26, 2010, www.libraryjournal.com/lj/communitybuildingandfacilities/884348-266/ pla_2010_conference_the_anythink.html.csp.

chapter eleven

Meller Langford and Roosevelt Weeks
with Dr. Rhea Brown Lawson

In the wake of Hurricane Ike
The Houston Public Library responds

When Hurricane Ike made landfall on September 12, 2008, packing winds in excess of 100 miles per hour, it became the third costliest hurricane ever to make landfall in the United States. It was the ninth named storm, fifth hurricane, and third major hurricane of the 2008 hurricane season and it was headed for Houston, Texas, the nation's fourth largest city.

Over two million Houston households, businesses, schools, and hospitals lost electricity. There was widespread property damage, and downed power lines caused the interruption of essential basic services. Schools, day care centers, and businesses were forced to close for several weeks. Downtown Houston shut down for three days in order for emergency workers to make sure that city buildings were safe, do major cleanup, restore traffic signals and telecommunications, bring basic city services back on line, and make available post-Ike emergency assistance.

Immediately after the hurricane, the Houston Public Library (HPL) director, Dr. Rhea Brown Lawson, announced that the library's total resources would be committed and accessible to assist the city's recovery efforts. Dr. Lawson emphasized that the library's core mission and responsibility in the wake of such devastation would be assisting the Houston community with healing and recovery efforts. She stated, "Our efforts will be led by the immediate need for compassion and caring for the Houston community and our staff."

Because a number of the HPL's library locations were significantly affected by Hurricane Ike, Lawson made the decision to concentrate the libraries' resources in a single location, the Central Library in downtown Houston, calling it "command

127

Dedicated workstations for FEMA claims, Houston Public Library. Photo courtesy Houston Public Library.

central." Four days after the hurricane, most of the library's staff from across the system's forty locations reported to the Central Library, which then opened its doors to the public. Because schools and day care agencies were closed, the staff members were allowed to bring their children to work with them. Lawson stated, "Our residents and our staff need a place to find some normalcy in the chaotic aftermath of Ike. They need a place to help them ensure their children that our community will be OK. The public library's role as a community gathering place and safe haven was never needed as much as right now."

The library staff quickly provided essential post-Ike disaster support to Houston's residents in three major ways: by establishing the Children's Zone in the Central Library, by deploying the library's mobile unit to communities hit hard by the storm, and by opening its community-based computer centers to provide Internet access, as well as assisting with FEMA (Federal Emergency Management Agency) forms and the Army Corps of Engineers' Blue Roof Assistance program. In addition, the staff restored core library services and programs at the Central Library.

Community-based disaster recovery services

Because the HPL has always been active in bringing library services and other programs to underserved parts of the city, two of its services were particularly

Houston Public Library's Mobile Express, a computer lab on wheels. Photo courtesy Houston Public Library.

well-positioned to be effective after the storm: HPL Mobile Express, a "computer lab on wheels"; and WeCAN community access locations, which are computer labs that provide citizens with free high-speed broadband Internet access located in community centers in high-need neighborhoods.

After Hurricane Ike hit the region, the HPL transformed these two services into mobile and community-based post-disaster recovery units. As the response from many other city departments was impaired because of the hurricane, HPL Mobile Express and WeCAN units provided communities most in need with access to social supports and services within walking distance of residents' homes.

The HPL's placement of computer access points, Internet resources, and trained staff both in neighborhoods and at the Central Library made the Library Disaster Recovery Support Centers a huge help to the city's residents, as they were quick and effective sources of assistance. The Library Disaster Recovery Support Centers provided residents with up-to-the-minute information on changing federal, state, and local disaster services and deadlines, such as the emergency points of distribution established to give out water, ice, and ready-to-eat meals.

The Library Disaster Recovery Support Centers continued to function well after the hurricane to address the continuing needs of the affected communities. The HPL Mobile Express unit was deployed at community centers around the city in areas that still did not have access to power and phone service. The HPL continued with recovery efforts for 45 days after the storm—whereas most other response efforts concluded after only a few weeks—providing Mobile Express and WeCAN services to more than 3,500 households and 10,700 residents, who otherwise might have received delayed assistance or no assistance at all.

The Houston Public Library was one of the 2008–2009 Public Technology Institute's Technology Solution award winners in the category of telecom and IT for its inventive approach to library solutions and post-disaster recovery efforts.

The Children's Zone

With the goal of recovering city services quickly, Mayor Bill White requested all emergency responders and essential workers to report to work immediately following the storm. Many of these individuals who had children were unable to report to work because schools and day cares were closed. Parents who had no alternative care for their children struggled with the dilemma of being asked to return to work while leaving their children home alone without electricity and supervision. Some municipal employees brought their children to work with them; but having children spend all day within city offices whose workers were performing essential post-disaster work was not a good solution.

When Mayor Pro Tem Sue Lovell became aware of this problem, she suggested to Rhea Lawson that the library coordinate a child services program to assist city employees with child care so that first responders and other essential employees could return to work. "It was a natural undertaking for us," said Lawson. "We have the appropriate resources and a staff that is flexible, quick-thinking, and highly skilled at organizing and with providing activities for children and teens. And it certainly helps that our electricity and air conditioning are working." The Children's Zone was a major example of how the Houston Public Library stepped up to the plate in response to a citywide need.

A team of children and teen services staff assumed leadership roles, establishing spaces in the Central Library as dedicated zones for different age-level activities. After receiving immediate approval by the mayor and City Council, the Children's Zone was operating within twenty-four hours of the mayor pro tem's call to Lawson. The following sections describe the steps the HPL team took to make this initiative successful.

Launching the Zone

Since all library staff systemwide reported to work at one location, there was a large and diverse pool of staff at all levels to support the quick execution of this initiative. The children and teen librarians had strong backgrounds in early childhood education, child development, adolescent literature, and early literacy. All levels of staff assisted with key components such as the registration process and ensuring the daily supply of food and drinks and other necessities.

Project coordinators leveraged the library's staff expertise, programs, resources, and services by (1) selecting staff with appropriate skill sets to lead or support the different age groups, and ensuring that there was an appropriate ratio of adults to children in the various aspects of the project; (2) overcoming the challenge of acquiring necessary resources and supplies ranging from food to baby wipes, given that the majority of stores and restaurants were closed; (3) providing appropriate programming for ages 5 to 18 and allocating program space; and (4) fine-tuning the project's logistics and schedule.

Citywide communication

The first official communication was a broadcast e-mail from the mayor pro tem promoting this emergency library child-care service to first responders and essential workers. Daily internal messages followed from the mayor and the library outlining these guidelines:

- the program is open to the first 250 school-aged children from the ages of 5 to 18 on a first-come, first-serve basis;
- registration and parent's city ID badges required;
- hours of operation from 8:00 a.m. to 5:30 p.m. until school districts and/ or day cares reopen;
- the library will provide activities and resources along with lunch and snacks daily; and
- the library would be unable to accommodate children who were ill, taking medicines, or had special needs.

The word spread quickly and city employees enthusiastically and gratefully responded to take advantage of this service.

Safety of children

From the outset of the initiative, parents were reassured that their children's safety and well-being were paramount. First, everyone knew that the facility offered a safe, secure environment, relaxing and comfortable space, and functioning air conditioning and lights. Second, the following security and safety measures were taken: (1) staff photocopied the parent's identification badge and added the parent's department and phone number; (2) one copy of the ID was attached to the registration form and the other copy served as part of the name tag for the nearly 500 children served; (3) the ID would be checked and matched again when the parent came to pick up the child; (4) staff escorted children in teams, depending on their age group, from the registration area to the appropriate program space.

Parents experienced a smooth, efficient, and friendly registration process and were encouraged to check on their child during the day. In a survey taken after the project ended, the quality of customer service for the Children's Zone was rated "Excellent" by 85 percent of the parents and "Very Good" by 15 percent. Quotes from the survey include:

"Exemplified exceptional customer service . . . very friendly staff. Way to go HPL!"

"I would like to thank everyone. You saved me from missing days at work."

Programming for multiple age groups (ages 5 to 9)

Two distinct program locations were used during the project, allowing younger children to be separated from older youth. A large programming space adjacent to the newly renovated Central Library's children's room provided child-sized tables and chairs; an easy-to-clean floor surface; and modern audiovisual equipment. This location was near restrooms, making it easy to monitor. The remodeled lower-level concourse meeting room appealed to the older youth, ages twelve and up, with built-in audiovisual equipment; striped, bold furnishings; and an area for showing movies or projecting video games. An adjacent room had a sink, small refrigerator, and storage area for serving snacks

Staff were keenly aware that the lives of these children had been disrupted by Hurricane Ike and that they did not have basic services at home; we knew therefore that they needed structure and a positive distraction because their circumstances and living conditions had changed dramatically. Thus, a structured daily routine—with story time, crafts, learning library resources, technology activities, and snacks—was provided.

Children's librarians and other staff assisted with improvising programming activities. The diversity of staff with multiple talents greatly contributed to the success of the project. Children's librarians conducted story times, crafts, daily exercise and dance sessions, and supervised play groups, while others did face painting or assisted with meals and bathroom breaks.

Programming activities were linked to literature and library resources. This provided added value for the children beyond what they might have experienced at a day-care facility. Children's books such as *Hurricane* by David Weisner and *Hurricane Hunters!: Riders on the Storm* by Chris Demarest, and nonfiction books such as *The Magic School Bus Inside a Hurricane* by Joanna Cole were shared to provide children with information and a framework for their experiences.

Another valuable activity was talking to the children about their hurricane experience and the impact at home. Children would talk about getting dressed in the dark and how it was hard to sleep at night because it was so hot. It was obvious through their stories that the children craved the normalcy of a pre-Ike schedule. Children's librarians improvised sleeping mats by using butcher paper, and if children didn't want to sleep they could color on their mats. The children's drawings often reflected their experiences with pictures of hurricanes and self-portraits.

The newly finished children's room added to the children's experience and offered a variety of books, CDs for afternoon aerobics, and a fun destination for children to browse for their own reading materials. Staff were eager to introduce children and parents to the new interactive gaming equipment designed to enhance decision-making and abstract-thinking skills, teamwork, and hand-eye coordination. With its captivating sights and sounds, the educational software at the early literacy station quickly became a magnet for younger children.

Tweens and teens (ages 10 to 18)

Programming for ages 10 to 18 provided a variety of recreational and social activities to keep the tweens and teens engaged, interested, and not have the Teen Zone simply act as a "holding" area. Many of these young people were worried about their home situation, and having a few hours of fun and interesting activities in their day was very therapeutic.

Teen librarians utilized ten Nintendo Wiis and ten small flat-screen TVs to provide interactive gaming activities for up to forty teens at a time. The Wii was a popular activity and an excellent icebreaker. The games required social interaction among several players, so the participants quickly made new friends.

In addition, a cart of materials from the extensive manga (Japanese graphic novels), books, and comic collection of the new Teen Room was available at all times in the Teen Zone. A few teens wanted to spend their entire time reading. WiFi access and the library's laptops gave them access to the library catalog and databases so they could browse and select their own materials.

The tweens and teens also explored the new MacBooks. They enjoyed experimenting with creating their own content by recording a video of themselves dancing or making pictures of themselves on Photo Booth. Of course, they also used the MacBooks to check their e-mail, update their MySpace/Facebook pages, and connect with friends (local or long distance) virtually. This was very popular since many of the youth did not have electricity in their homes.

During "unplug" periods when the electronic games were shut down, the youths played board games or read. By the time the relief effort ended, most tweens and teens felt they had a new group of friends and a new place to add to their routine: the library.

How the Houston Public Library benefited

This experience instilled in staff and in city residents a higher level of respect for the library's services and expertise. Library staff systemwide worked together for the first time in one environment. The experience fostered respect for the contributions made by all levels of staff and created a team that remained flexible and rose to any challenge presented. The library's contributions toward the city's recovery process enhanced the organization's public image among Houston residents and its role as a community anchor and vital institution.

Outcomes

By providing child care services for nearly 500 Houston area youth, 217 essential Houston city government workers from twenty-five different departments were able to return immediately to work, contributing to the Hurricane Ike recovery effort. Emergency 911 and City Call Center 311 employees were available to answer calls, Public Works and Engineering staff were able to work on traffic lights and clear debris, the General Services Division was able to inspect buildings for storm damage and begin repairs, and Houston police officers and firemen were available to assist where needed. Here are some comments from city employees who used the Children's Zone:

> This is a tardy but heartfelt message of thanks to everyone who dreamed up and put into action the post-hurricane program for children of employees at the library. We loved it! My child loved coming downtown with me and learning about the library—not to mention all the snacks and activities. I loved having her so close, well-cared for, and creatively occupied during the day.

> There had been stories in the newspaper about firms providing daycare for employees' children, but I assumed that was only for places where the staff could bill hundreds of dollars per hour. I was so touched by the City's operation and amazed that it was up and running and publicized and grateful we were able to get a spot. I still can't believe it was free of charge. It was just a blessing for me and my family in so many ways.

Children from thirteen area school districts returned to school sharing "library" stories as part of their "I survived" experience. The Zone heightened public awareness of the HPL's twenty-first-century library services and programs. Children and their parents were exposed to current, upgraded technologies. Many had not been in a library in years and were thrilled to see how the HPL had changed and what the library had to offer. The Houston Public Library gained new library users, causing the library card registration rate to increase by 15 percent.

The Children's Zone project generated great media exposure. A local TV station showed the children on the five o'clock news during a story-time session. Teens were filmed proudly displaying a large "Thank You, Dr. Lawson!" banner that they created. Lawson appeared on a popular live local TV program, *Great Day Houston*.

The Children's Zone won the 2009 Wayne Williams Library Project of the Year Award from the Texas Library Association for its contribution to recovery efforts after Ike.

Conclusions

For at least eight hours a day, while Houston's emergency workers and other essential staff worked to make sure their city recovered from a major crisis, their children were in a well-lit, air conditioned, safe environment, recovering a sense of security and balance in their lives through the structure of the program. Meanwhile, the HPL'S home page provided extensive links to hurricane-related information, and the HPL essentially transformed itself into a disaster recovery support operation. It is important to keep in mind that during this time, many HPL employees were also living without electricity, phone service, and water in their homes, and many had homes that had suffered significant hurricane damage. It was amazing to see the staff unite as a powerful team to give much-needed service to others, and how they themselves gained strength and found deep satisfaction in playing a vital role in the citywide recovery efforts. The 3 R's (relief, recovery, and renewal) became a key tenet embraced by Houston Public Library staff, allowing them to deliver extraordinary service during an extraordinary time.

chapter twelve

Matthew Evan Havens and Michael Dudley

Public libraries, peak oil, and climate change

T ry to envision running a complex institution like a public library system with oil prices approaching $200 per barrel. What would that mean for the library's budget in terms of fueling a fleet of trucks as well as the added cost of procuring new materials—to say nothing of ensuring that staff are able to afford to arrive at work? Or else imagine your community managing in a climate where the average daytime temperature is three degrees Celsius (about five degrees Fahrenheit) higher.[1] Even worse—the evenings no longer cool significantly to give people a reprieve from the daytime heat. This will have the most impact on the elderly and infirm, especially when the energy to run air conditioning is scarce or unaffordable, or electrical grids break down or fail altogether. Three degrees may sound insignificant, but averaged over the year, this increase leads to longer heat waves and contributes to more extreme weather events. If your public library manages to keep its air conditioning running, how will they cope with surging demand for respite, especially on the part of those unable to afford exorbitant energy bills?

The twin threats of climate change and energy scarcity are going to be among the greatest challenges the next few generations will have to face. Whether we consider emergency response and preparedness, our economies, our governance, or in particular our built environments and infrastructure, we are facing the prospect of a new "normal" about which we have little certainty, but for which we must nonetheless prepare, and at the governmental, institutional, business, and household levels.

Already, many people live in communities that have seen evident shifts in the climate: earlier springs, later autumns, less snow, or rain that comes all at once instead of spread out over the season. Extreme weather events are occurring with such frequency they are almost becoming normal. These are the twin crises that human society is now facing—peak oil (or more generally, energy scarcity) and climate change. Many informed observers have predicted that current conventional oil production has already reached or is currently at its peak. Essentially, we have used half of the world's nonrenewable resources of oil, and access to the second half will be more difficult, will fail to meet ever-growing demand, and will contribute to geopolitical instability.[2]

This unraveling of conditions long accepted as normal and permanent poses a significant challenge to planning, whether for cities, businesses, or large institutions such as public libraries. We are accustomed to basing our planning on the assumed continuity into the future of relative stability, including dependable economic growth, reliable supplies of resources, and geopolitical stability. Most of our assumptions concerning these foundations will likely be called into question as we progress from the old "normal" to a new one—whatever that may be. What the specific details of such a planning context will be may be difficult to predict. Yet a "post-carbon" world without affordable and accessible fossil fuels is almost certain to require us to downscale and re-localize almost everything we do: to strengthen our economies on a local and regional scale, to source more of our food and goods locally, and to rediscover the resources and knowledge that we have within ourselves and our communities to be more self-reliant.

As with many industries and institutions within metropolitan areas, public library systems are highly complex and energy-intensive operations dependent on flows of materials both internal and external. Their lifeblood—books—are manufactured globally, their paper originating in forests accessed by diesel-fueled trucks, or recycling plants. On a daily basis trucks also ferry materials between branches, and library facilities generate significant greenhouse gases by drawing patrons arriving in cars. The power supplies of most libraries depend upon highly centralized municipal and regional power grids utilizing a combination of coal, hydroelectric, nuclear power, and natural gas. Libraries are also heavily reliant on telecommunication networks, Web-based data, and cloud storage, which themselves draw on this same massive but rapidly-aging and vulnerable power infrastructure.[3]

The public libraries of a post-carbon world will be different in many ways, but will still serve the same fundamental role as always: as depositories of community, regional, and local culture, history, and knowledge. Public libraries stand to be significantly affected by a peak-oil age but have the potential to contribute to their communities' transition to a post-carbon world.

Our predicament

In his book *The Long Descent*, John Michael Greer points out that the combined threats of energy scarcity and climate change are a *predicament* as opposed to a *problem*. The two are very different: problems can be eliminated with solutions, and one can thus move on; a predicament can only be responded to and will not go away.[4] It is the nature and scale of the responses that we choose to cope with our predicament that will measure our success as communities in the future. We must start to carefully consider what responses and actions we will take before we feel the full effect of these predicaments.

Just about every part of our current lifestyle is subsidized by inexpensive fossil fuels, mainly oil. As the easy-to-reach and extract (and thus cheap) fossil fuels start to run out, the oil industry is turning to the riskier, dirtier, and more expensive sources. The age of oil gushing out of the ground is long over; today oil companies seek new supplies in risky deepwater ventures or mine it out of the ground, leaving lasting environmental damage. Hence the deepwater drilling in the Gulf of Mexico which resulted in the Deepwater Horizon oil spill of 2010 and the controversial increase in the destructive and excessive carbon-emitting production of bitumen from the tar sands in Canada.

The double predicament of our carbon-intensive way of life based on fossil fuels is that we will eventually run out of them, but not before they irreparably change our climate. Indeed, climate scientists have been repeatedly surprised over the past decade as studies and evidence indicate that the climate may be changing much quicker than originally expected. Internationally accepted predictions upon which climate and energy policies are based have turned out to be incorrect and conservative: arctic ice melt, sea level rise, and temperature increases are happening much sooner and faster than originally predicted.[5]

Every few years we hear about a new "source" of energy or technology that will save us from our predicament—be it hydrogen-fueled cars, biofuels like corn ethanol, "clean" coal, or the more recent expansion of shale natural gas production via "fracking" in North America. But all of these promised energy solutions come with their own hidden drawbacks, barriers, and unintended consequences.

Hydrogen is essentially not an energy source but an energy carrier and may be prohibitively expensive and inefficient to utilize beyond specialized uses. Ethanol production from corn is a highly inefficient way to produce a liquid transport fuel, considering the total energy in the form of tractor diesel fuel, fertilizer, pesticides, natural gas, and electricity that must be invested to produce, harvest, and convert the crop to fuel, not to mention the controversial redirection of food crops from mouths to fuel tanks. So-called "clean" coal in the form of carbon capture and storage is in the testing and demonstration phase only and will also be costly for the coal industry to implement, requiring a vast new infrastructure for transporting and burying the carbon that is captured.[6] The recent rapid expansion of drilling for "shale gas" in North America and its contribution to current low gas prices is seen by some to be unsustainable, not to mention threatening to local water tables and environmentally destructive.[7]

Even renewable energy technologies have their drawbacks and limitations if we are to look to them to get us out of our twin fixes. Renewable energy sources will certainly play a vital role in our future energy mix; however, technologies like wind and solar still only contribute a very small amount to our energy requirements (although they are among the fastest-growing sectors). North America's largest renewable energy sector is hydroelectric dams, and most of the sufficient sites for large-scale dams have been developed already. Even a substantial increase in renewable energy technology will not be able to replace oil.[8] The harvesting of raw materials and fabrication of solar photovoltaic panels, for example, is an extremely energy-intensive process that is itself currently dependent upon fossil fuels to be feasible. The rare earth elements that many of these advanced technologies require are also found in few places on earth (e.g., China), and increasing demand will quickly strain limited supplies. The ultimate test and question for these technologies is: can they power their own future production? Could a windmill installation, for example, ever provide enough energy to be able to fully manufacture new windmills? Current costs, efficiencies, and the intermittency of these sources indicate that this may not be possible.

Ramping up any new energy technology or production will take enormous amounts of money and time and neither business nor government seem wholly committed to the effort that it will take, rather paying lip service to visions of a cleaner and more efficient future. We've been hearing about electric and hydrogen cars for almost fifteen years now, yet even hybrid vehicles that still use gasoline (albeit at much greater efficiencies) still only make up a small fraction of the vehicle fleet. It seems these efficient technologies still remain in the realm of the rich and trendy; the zero-emission vehicle for the common person is still a long way off. Indeed, building the sufficient infrastructure for an energy system or systems to replace the current one to prepare for the shock that may happen when oil scarcity is felt will take decades. It has been recommended that these preparations must be started at least ten to twenty years prior to the onset of peak oil, just to prevent significant economic disruptions.[9] Unfortunately, in many regions the evidence of any consensus on how to proceed on a transition is lacking.

Despite recent discussion and efforts to move to energy-efficient design and construction when planning our communities, fundamental inefficiencies exist in our living and work spaces, and these inefficiencies continue to be built into them. We build extra-large houses with poor building envelopes and then outfit them with large central heating and cooling units; we heat and cool the entire house while many of the rooms go unused for large parts of the day; we use a lot of money, energy, and infrastructure in order to carry our bodily wastes out of our homes in potable water; we continue to subsidize private automobile use with tax-funded roads and bridges, encouraging people to commute to work alone in large vehicles, providing the illusion of convenience and to display our individual economic achievement.

We have heard from many scientists and activists that this is unsustainable, and even some heads of state have admitted that we are addicted to oil.[10] Rob Hopkins in his *Transition Handbook* explores this idea further and says that, just like any other addict that relies on a substance to function, so it is with us and oil. When a person is dependent on a substance, thinking about discontinuing use of that substance, or even considering cutting back, can cause fear and discomfort. A substance that an addict is reliant upon can pose a hazard to their future well-being; this is true with fossil fuels and climate change. It also can be harmful to us while we are using it, which we certainly see with pollution, detrimental health effects, and environmental destruction.[11]

The potential range of post-carbon planning issues is enormous—and can only be touched on here—but would include identifying and securing usable agricultural land, securing alternative and low-energy means of transporting people and supplies, and provisioning emergency shelter, especially in extreme climates. What is certain is that the dramatic "re-localization" that will be necessary (local power supplies, gardening, and support networks) will mean a new kind of local polity and decision making that will be more vigorous and more necessary than the rather passive democracy with which most of us are familiar. This transition will demand that we look closer to home—and within ourselves—for new resources.

Public libraries and "transition"

If we are to successfully downscale and localize our economies, to "re-skill" ourselves to be more self-reliant, and source our foodstuffs and clothing regionally, the public library will have a significant role to play. In the first mainstream treatment of this topic in the library literature, Debra J. Slone in the March 2008 issue of *Library Journal* speculated how the public library will be affected by peak oil. Most of the article relates to an expected surge in reference questions on self-reliance, as people are no longer able to afford what they used to purchase, are unable to travel to acquire those goods, or goods are simply unavailable locally. She writes,

> Librarians will have to locate and provide information about local resources for food, medicine, travel, and shelter. They will be required to identify local talent and experts and list plants native to the area. They will carry information about the environmental needs of the region, its transportation and the source of the community's water, and whether it is healthy. Libraries will have to maintain current travel information (walking, bus, car, golf cart, etc.) and knowledge about local land use. Librarians will also identify and address barriers to information access. They will facilitate local access to people developing alternative means of transportation, energy, and more. They will keep track of available housing and whether there is enough of it. Armed with data about the resources that make communities function, librarians can begin to develop an information, communication, and referral system that addresses the unique needs and assets of their region.[12]

A connection with our region and gaining a thorough, pragmatic, and practical knowledge base concerning its capabilities to support human community is a specialty wherein the contributions and capabilities of the public library will prove particularly valuable. As Kirkpatrick Sale describes in his 1991 book *Dwellers in the Land*, to gain a sense of one's region and become true "dwellers in the land" we must

> relearn the laws of [nature], to come to know the earth fully and honestly, [and to] understand place, the immediate specific place where

we live. The kinds of soils and rocks under our feet; the source of the waters we drink; the meaning of the different kinds of winds; the common insects, birds, mammals, plants, and trees; the particular cycles of the seasons; the times to plant and harvest and forage—these are the things that are necessary to know. The limits of its resources; the carrying capacities of its lands and waters; the places where it must not be stressed; the places where its bounties can best be developed; the treasure it holds and the treasure it withholds—these are the things that must be understood.[13]

Libraries will need to become the depositories and collection point of what Sale refers to as the lore of the land, which may be forgotten but relearnable. This role is already being fulfilled at some public libraries. For example, the Calgary Public Library's "Living Library" service allows a library patron to "borrow" a local person for the purpose of conversation and knowledge-sharing. The success of this initiative speaks to the need for this lost lore.[14] In a post-carbon world it is easy to see how, eventually, the knowledge of community experts and elders would be in such high demand that the distribution of their expertise would need to be managed by the library.

"Transition" plans (which may appear under a variety of names including post-carbon cities, post-peak, and so on) and actions to make communities more resilient have been undertaken by communities large and small, mainly in the United Kingdom and North America. Transition plans consider ways in which a given community—and its networks of businesses, institutions, organizations, and individuals—can become more self-reliant based on its own resources, and by developing its own capacities through new economic relationships and building up the community's skill base. Much of this planning started with concerned citizens or members of existing community groups and has evolved into taking local initiatives on preparing for peak oil. These initiatives have had varying success collaborating with local governments in implementing their plans. Many of these movements began with a focus on local food production and have expanded to planning energy and transport alternatives, re-skilling, and knowledge sharing.[15]

Transition Town Totnes in the United Kingdom is one of the pioneering communities that are taking action to prepare for energy scarcity and climate change. Totnes has inspired other community movements and an international network for transition initiatives, and has been a source for some of the early writing on the subject, such as Rob Hopkins's *The Transition Handbook* and Shaun Camberlin's *The Transition Timeline*. Hundreds of people have visited the town to undertake "transition training." The town and its people have reduced individual and community emissions, installed small-scale renewable energy production, planted food crops, and taken steps to share skill-based knowledge around the community.[16]

Re-skilling will become an important activity for many people in their daily lives. Few city dwellers today have the know-how to grow their own food, repair even the simplest technologies, or sew their own clothes. As Debra Slone suggests, assisting community members in accessing such information will be a vital public library function as cheap energy supplies dwindle. Having multiple knowledge sets and robust ways to pass that knowledge along to fellow community members will be an important part of a resilient community, and one which the public library is ideally situated to provide.

Library functions themselves will, however, be affected by energy disruptions. New investment in energy-efficient building materials and power plants will need to be made, and are already under way in many jurisdictions. The Bronx Library Center, for example, in 2007 became the first public LEED (Leadership in Energy and Environmental Design) Silver building in New York City, and a number of other public libraries (Seattle, Minneapolis, Fayetteville) have also constructed or renovated to LEED or other energy-efficiency standards.[17] The Pennsville Public Library in New Jersey has not only installed solar panels, but is selling electricity back to the grid, which utility customers can purchase—providing the library with a new revenue stream.[18] Another innovative solution is District Energy, which utilizes a central combined heat and power plant to provide heat, cooling, and hot water to multiple buildings, resulting in significant energy savings and greenhouse gas reductions. This was the energy infrastructure chosen in 2009 for the revitalized downtown Hamilton Public Library in Hamilton, Ontario, which will be sharing its connection to the system with a farmer's market, city hall, and the Board of Education.[19]

Reductions in the energy-intensity of other library operations may be required. For example, the inter-branch shipping of materials might need to be scaled down in frequency and shifted to electric fleets. In the spring of 2010 FedEx—already a leader in hybrid-electric vans—announced that it was going to start using small all-electric delivery vans.[20] Even human-powered cargo bikes might be feasible for the needs of smaller library branches in communities with relatively modest changes in elevation. There is a surging interest in human-powered vehicles for business purposes, utilizing cargo bikes to fill the need for transporting goods too large for bike couriers but not requiring a full truck.[21]

As suggested in the opening paragraphs, however, the oncoming changes brought about by energy depletion or intolerable weather may impose new pressures on libraries to meet the needs of people unable to heat or cool their homes. As such, libraries—more than ever—will need to assert their role as an essential service, so as to be provided with the resources (including power supplies) needed to meet these demands.

There is one aspect of twenty-first-century library service that stands to be significantly challenged in an energy-poor future: access to databases, cloud storage, and online networking. As Adrian Atkinson suggests in his remarkable trilogy of articles "Cities after Oil," the peak oil era may also be one of "peak information":

> Most of what today is considered to be "information" will disappear— for three reasons. Firstly, much information today is only available electronically and with the failure of electrical systems this will disappear through the illegibility of electronic memories. Secondly, most of what is deemed to be useful today by way of knowledge and information will lose its relevance and so be abandoned. And finally, making a living through developing and processing knowledge will become a luxury

in so far as most human time will return to manual work in fields and workshops. One can imagine, if there is some planning for an energy- (and knowledge-) parsimonious future, that some centres (universities or whatever) will survive and these will rescue and store information and go on to recover or re-learn knowledge relevant to the emergent circumstances.[22]

It may be hard to believe that we in the "Information Age" could see its dissolution. Yet there would appear a very real possibility that all those innumerable bytes of data we now take for granted may well be lost as our society powers down. It may make Nicholson Baker's admonitions in *Double Fold*—a condemnation of microfilming, digitization, and the disposal of paper in libraries—seem particularly prescient.[23] Libraries of all kinds may wish to reconsider their rush to digitize and discard paper sources, for there may be a time when their electronic counterparts fail.

If peak oil theorists and transition advocates are correct, and our cities and economies will need to "power down," then public libraries will need to carefully reassess their own operations, facilities, and programming so that they will be capable of maintaining their functioning under extraordinarily straitened circumstances. But in such circumstances, it is clear that public libraries will be more important to their communities than ever, to provide the information and guidance needed to conserve, preserve, and re-skill for a warmer and low-energy future.

Further reading

For an excellent description of the economics of peak oil and the resultant "oscillating decline," see David Korowicz, "On the Cusp of Collapse: Complexity, Energy and the Globalized Economy," in *Fleeing Vesuvius*, ed. Richard Douthwaite and Gillian Fallon (Garbriola Island: New Society, 2011).

For a vision of how education may change in America in a post-peak world, see James Howard Kunstler, *The Long Emergency* (New York: Atlantic Monthly, 2005); and Nancy Lee Wood. "Community Colleges," in *The Post Carbon Reader*, ed. Richard Heinberg and Daniel Lerch (Healdsburg: Watershed Media, 2010).

NOTES

1. This is the estimate according to the Intergovernmental Panel on Climate Change, www.ipcc.ch/publications_and_data/ar4/syr/en/spms3.html.

2. For a comprehensive resource on peak oil predictions and forecasting, see the Association for the Study of Peak Oil at www.peakoil.net.

3. Jason Makansi, *Lights Out: The Electricity Crisis, the Global Economy and What It Means to You* (New York: Wiley, 2007).

4. John Michael Greer, *The Long Descent* (Gabriola Island: New Society, 2008), 22.

5. Bill McKibben, *Eaarth* (Toronto: Alfred A. Knopf Canada, 2010), 14–15.

6. A consensus is building among energy experts that no single energy source will be able to effectively replace oil. See especially Richard Heinberg, *Searching for a Miracle: Net Energy Limits and the Fate of Industrial Society* (San Francisco: International Forum on Globalization and the Post Carbon Institute, 2009); Vaclav Smil, *Energy Myths and Realities* (Washington: AEI, 2010).

7. See the recent Post Carbon Institute report by J. David Hughes, *Will Natural Gas Fuel the 21st Century?* (Post Carbon Institute, 2011).

8. Heinberg, *Searching for a Miracle*.

9. The first report on peak oil prepared for the U.S. Department of Energy raises concern about the time it will take to prepare for peak oil. Robert Hirsch and others, *Peaking of World Oil Production: Impacts, Mitigation, & Risk Management* (2005). See also Richard Heinberg, *The Party's Over* (Gabriola Island: New Society, 2005).

10. For example, President George W. Bush's (in)famous declaration in 2006 that America was "addicted to oil."

11. Rob Hopkins, *The Transition Handbook* (Totnes: Green Books, 2008).

12. Debra J. Slone, "After Oil," *Library Journal* 133, no. 5 (2008): 28–31.

13. Kirkpatrick Sale, *Dwellers in the Land* (Gabriola Island: New Society, 1991), 42.

14. See the Calgary Public Library, "Living Library," http://blog.calgarypubliclibrary.com/blogs/volunteers/pages/living-library.aspx.

15. For a recent summary on municipal government peak-oil actions, see Daniel Lerch, *Post Carbon Cities: Planning for Energy and Climate Uncertainty* (Sebastopol: Post Carbon, 2007); and for transition towns, see Hopkins, *The Transition Handbook*.

16. Transition Town Totnes, www.transitiontowntotnes.org/home.

17. "Green Library," *Wikipedia*, http://en.wikipedia.org/wiki/Green_library.

18. "Pennsville Library Goes Green," Pennsville Public Library, www.pennsvillelibrary.org/index.php.

19. "Hamilton Community Energy: Single Source Provider of Integrated District Energy Solutions," www.hamiltonce.com/.

20. Jimmy Mengel, "FedEx Rolls Out All-Electric Delivery Vans," *Green Chip Stocks*, March 31, 2010, www.greenchipstocks.com/articles/fedex-all-electric-delivery-vans/865.

21. Sarah Elton, "Small Businesses Turning to Pedal Power," *The Globe and Mail*, June 15, 2011, www.theglobeandmail.com/report-on-business/small-business/start/business-planning/small-businesses-turning-to-pedal-power/article2061678/.

22. Adrian Atkinson, "Cities After Oil–3: Collapse and the Fate of Cities," *City* 12, no. 1 (2008): 87.

23. Nicholson Baker, *Double Fold: Libraries and the Assault on Paper* (New York: Vintage, 2002).

chapter thirteen

Innocent Chirisa

Collaborative community library planning and economic crisis
The case of Harare, Zimbabwe

Between 1890 and 1902 public libraries were founded in Harare, as well as in the cities of Bulawayo, Gweru, and Mutare. They continue to contribute to socioeconomic development in their cities by complementing the efforts of formal educational institutions, and by investing in training, capacity building, and by encouraging the development of appropriate skills, all of which are fundamental for poverty reduction. Harare is a city with a rapidly growing population and hence increasing demand for information. Members of the community engaged in self-help projects like small business ventures utilize the library to gain access to newspapers and information relating to income generation and business management.

However, Harare's libraries face considerable financial, staffing, and materials constraints, while the city itself is facing a number of environmental, economic, and social challenges including climate change, poverty, financial constraints, and political and security disorders, as well as corruption and economic instability, to mention a few.

Investing in public libraries in Africa is often downplayed in favor of other challenges and priorities seen as more pressing. In Zimbabwe, however, there has been a realization by government that investment in education at all levels—primary, secondary, and tertiary levels—is important towards the future sustainability of the nation. This policy realization has seen the introduction and development of these institutions since the country got its independence in 1980.

It must be noted, though, that the colonial educational policy was skewed in favor of the white minority, such that very little investment was made towards the African majority.[1] In the first decade of independence, Zimbabwe invested a lot in the development and construction of primary and secondary schools, with those in rural areas being the most favored. As John Welford recounts in his overview of the development of Zimbabwe's libraries, this was done to correct a historic neglect, in which only the small, white ruling population enjoyed well-stocked public libraries. Following independence in 1980, however, the new government, upon hiring a consultant, determined that, since 90 percent of the population was rural and disadvantaged and had no access to libraries, this is where the government's library service priorities should be.[2] However, due to a rapid increase in urbanization since then, the need has partly shifted to urban areas as well.

The second decade after independence saw a kind of shift toward tertiary (post-secondary) education development, and a number of universities emerged. Nevertheless, the number of corresponding libraries was far below the expectation. Given the traditional public library role of supporting formal education, this has proved a serious barrier to tertiary education delivery, not only in terms of physical facilities but in the quality of materials, as well as other incidental requirements which make reading and a culture of reading possible. Even in the primary and education sector, the recent collapse of the economy (1997–2009) has led to the compromise of standards as a huge number of teachers and pupils alike have sought refuge in private schools and colleges offering better remuneration and education, respectively.[3]

In the area of information and communication technology (ICT) facilities, the main challenge is electricity service, which is subject to rolling blackouts almost daily. Not only is it a question of power, but the computers are still grossly inadequate. Of the public school system it has been remarked, "the majority of the schools do not have the basic facilities required for the use of computer technology."[4] In his research on public libraries in sub-Saharan Africa, Chisenga also notes that because of barriers such as the shortage of computers, a lack of funds, and an absence of ICT skills, few library services in sub-Saharan Africa have been able to take advantage of ICT facilities to extend digital information service for the benefit of their communities.[5] Although a large number of public libraries in developed countries are using the Web to provide access to a wide variety of information resources and services, including online community information, access to databases, online reservation of library materials, and many other services, this is not yet the case in most public libraries in sub-Saharan Africa. While the idea of e-learning is dominating practice the world over, this is still decades away from full realization with respect to public library needs.

In spite of these challenges, public libraries in Africa—as elsewhere—are a living force for community development, serving all users irrespective of race, class, or gender. As critical gateways for knowledge creation, diffusion, and advancement, public libraries provide free access to information in order to serve an educational role in the broadest sense. However, a lack of resources can affect this noble objective; in some cases existing libraries are in a sorry state of dilapidation due to neglect and lack of investment during the country's "lost decade" in the economic sector.

Harare and its public libraries

Harare is the capital city of Zimbabwe and its largest city. The city can basically be divided into three subregions—the Central, Northern (predominantly former white suburbs), and Western regions (mostly former African townships—see map below). The city is expanding at a very fast rate, and it is estimated that Greater Harare (including its satellite towns of Ruwa, Epworth, Chitungwiza, and Christon Bank) has a population of more than 3 million inhabitants.

The Harare City Library dates back to the colonial era and has a network of five libraries in the low-density residential areas (High-Income Areas, or HIAs) of the city (Mount Pleasant, Greendale, Highlands, Mabelreign, and Hatfield). These are all administered by the Queen Victoria Memorial Library, now known as Harare City Library. The second typology of libraries is the Low-Income Areas' (LIA) libraries, which are managed by the City Council under the city's Department of Housing and Community Services (DHCS). The city of Harare operates a total of ten libraries in the former African townships, and these are centrally administered from the Highfield Central Library. Municipal library systems are administered by the municipality's community service department. Unfortunately, attempts to amalgamate the two public library systems have been unsuccessful, mostly due to the fact that the two systems have different historical backgrounds deeply rooted in the policies of separate development.

The Harare City Library was established through an Act of Parliament known as the Queen Victoria Memorial Library Act of 1902. After the country's inde-

Map of Harare, Zimbabwe. Courtesy Office of the Surveyor-General, City of Harare.

pendence in 1980, the library was renamed the Harare City Library through the promulgation of the Harare City Library Act of 1982. Significantly, this act is silent on who has the responsibility for funding the Harare City Library; while the library did receive grants from the government, these ceased in 1995. From that date the library has relied on subscriptions, fines, and donations from well-wishers as well as grants from the local authorities.

Registration to be a member of a Harare library (Low-Income Areas, LIA) requires that the applicant bring with him or her a National Identity Card, a Current Statement of Water and Electricity, and a two-dollar (U.S.) "Joining fee," which also becomes a subscription per month of four dollars if one intends to borrow books. It is also a requirement that one is a resident in the defined local area (for example, Mufakose Library caters to residents of Mufakose, Budiriro, and Marimba). In the (High-Income Area) Harare City Library system, a non-refundable registration fee of ten dollars (U.S.) is paid by an individual on joining in order to be a member. A student identification card is required for entry and registration, while pensioners are given a 10 percent discount on all charges. The fees paid under Harare City (HIA) libraries are quite a bit higher than those paid under the (LIA) City of Harare libraries, as they are the funds used for the maintenance of the library.

Poorer residents cannot generally afford these high subscription fees and fines, nor the transport costs often incurred to get to a library. Compounding this barrier is the fact that the library collection does not take into consideration the needs of illiterate or semi-illiterate, physically and mentally disadvantaged users, thus creating a situation of social exclusion. Mataraso has noted that

> information [is] denied people who cannot read English; who have already been failed by the education system; whose lives are so constrained by poverty as to make the question of reading, or even thinking beyond immediate problem solving, remote. It must be time to look at a radical redevelopment of the library system which can ensure access to information, understanding and knowledge for all.[6]

Some public libraries provide services to the visually and physically disadvantaged through working with special libraries that have specialized resources and equipment for such groups (e.g., by providing the Dorothy Duncan Library for the Blind, Emerald Hill School for the blind and deaf, and the Jairos Jiri Centre). The Dorothy Duncan Library provides library services without any discrimination, for example, print material in Braille format, audiotapes, and CDs.

Challenges facing Harare's public libraries

It should be noted that a decade of economic crisis has left few effective distinctions between the HIA and LIA—and their libraries. The economy is in shambles following the country's involvement between 1998 and 2002 in the war in the Democratic Republic of the Congo, which cost hundreds of millions of dollars; a disastrous and corrupt process of "agrarian reforms," which saw formerly productive lands providing export crops go to political and military insiders who were largely incapable of (or uninterested in) cultivating them; and years of hyperinflation that resulted in the government suspending its own currency. Unemployment is in excess of 90 percent, and government spending is nearly 98 percent of GDP.[7]

As a result of this crisis, Harare's public libraries, especially those operated by the City of Harare, are suffering from serious financial constraints. This has stifled information provision; money to buy new books is difficult to come by, as they have thus far depended on fees and donations from donor agencies such as Book Aid International and United States Information Services. Most of the outdated materials the libraries harbor have proved to be of very little use to the users. Old Mutual, a private corporation, has helped with the establishment of an Internet café at one of the libraries and users pay a fee of U.S. one dollar per hour. Harare library does not own any computers; it uses an outdated card and loan system known as the Browne Issue system.[8]

The other challenge deriving from severe financial constraints is related to low staffing levels: Harare City Library has only two librarians, and in the other branches they only have one each. This makes it difficult to manage the day-to-day activities in the library.[9] In keeping with this observation, Chisenga has pointed out that the major barriers to the use of ICTs in the Zimbabwean public library system are insufficient funding from government and a lack of appropriate training of staff.[10] ICT equipment is expensive, making it difficult for public libraries to budget for its purchase from their own funds; for this reason, many public libraries have failed to purchase even a single computer from their own funds. In contrast, the public libraries' manual card catalog and Browne charging system provide an effective means of operating the library, and no major advantage is seen by staff in automating these functions, as fairly frequent electricity supply cuts are seen as a major threat to any automated system.

Another challenge is that of facilities dilapidation due to lack of maintenance. Public libraries have been neglected and can do with an urgent facelift. Many feature broken windows; dysfunctional toilets; bookshelves that are in a shambles; tattered and torn books (most of them missing pages or having torn covers). Some of the academic textbooks have become irrelevant and have since been superseded by newer editions, and the authorities are failing to restock. The Glen Norah Library used to be filled with students from schools in the high-density suburb jostling for space, and it was common to see people queuing all day waiting for their turn to use the facility. A stroll on the premises now shows that the library has lost its glamour and is fast becoming a white elephant. With a new open-air club having been established nearby, one is welcomed by the stench from the nearby bush where revelers relieve themselves. One official to whom I spoke, who has worked at the library for more than fifteen years, said the library had since lost its glory and the new student generation was shunning the facility, owing to outdated, tattered books and a lack of computers for library users.

The deprived state of Harare's public libraries represents a significant disadvantage to its citizens. The current knowledge-driven economy requires public libraries to develop sustainable ways to ensure that they remain in sync with the demand of their dynamic environments.[11] Existing libraries need to be renovated and furnished with new literature reflecting current curriculum needs so that students are not disadvantaged by outdated literature ranging from the 1950s to the 1990s. To address the intermittent power supply and enable more dependable ICT services, communities need help investing in low-cost, distributed, and renewable energy technologies, including diesel-powered generators and solar energy. And to reduce transportation costs for low-income library users, additional public library subsidiaries should be located in almost every neighborhood.

However, given economic constraints, a different approach is needed. More awareness needs to be created among civil society, the private sector, and nongovernmental organizations concerning the critical need for establishing and investing in public library development, maintenance, and expansion. Community stakeholders and members should be given a greater role in supporting and planning these facilities and their services. At present there are no partnerships in place with other actors because the city of Harare has a monopoly on the supply of library services.

A community participatory/collaborative model

A community led model for library development could contribute to the creation of better linkages and relations with all stakeholders in the community, including local government, schools, universities, businesses, farmers, publishers, writers, booksellers, research institutions, and nongovernmental organizations. Public–private partnerships (P3s) are partnerships between public sector organizations like libraries and public and private sector businesses. These partnerships are being used as a platform to develop infrastructure and deliver public services on a cost-effective and sustainable basis, developing and sharing good practices, and sharing each other's networks and linkages. Nhema reports that discussions are under way to explore local business support for libraries in Harare.[12]

There are some library services for which a P3 approach would work very well. The demand for Internet access is very high, and there are now many Internet cafes in the city center. Working with local businesses would help fund, sponsor, and equip Internet facilities at each library, which would satisfy user needs and also enable libraries to generate some revenue. There are specialized academic and nongovernmental libraries in the city with which partnerships might also be possible. The underlying principle of a community participatory/collaborative model is for inclusivity to encourage more equitable and effective information provision and advancement.

The diagram at right is a suggested community model for the enhancement of public libraries in Harare. It is a series of interrelated and interconnected steps organized at three basic levels: the neighborhood, the municipality, and the subarea (region). It must start with comprehensive community awareness campaigns on the importance of libraries, knowledge generation, and information retrieval and usage. The City Council should facilitate and support community-based participatory planning, learning, and action which could help in solidifying

community-public provate partnership and strategic alliances. This step feeds into a participatory budgeting process which has the effect of increasing voice and space for community actors in establishing a variety of menas for creative revenue generation. Once this is in place, some collaborative fundraising (building on enhanced public-private partnerships) assists in consolidating community stewardship. The community must feel that it owns the process and the assets that come through it.

Community stakeholders and members should participate in library capacity-building efforts, including those related to training and staff development. Combined with participatory planning and budgeting, this then leads to informed procurement and materials acquisition (books, computers, desks, shelves) and reinforces community oversight—that is, participatory monitoring and evaluation of library performance by community members.

This model would enhance local governance and hence, trust, accountability, and the library's role in improving social justice in communities. In these proposed steps (which are not necessarily linear but iterative and interactive) lie the prospects for greater resilience and sustainability in the city's library programs. An inclusive approach to library development, maintenance, and usage such as this may encourage a practice of community building in which the library serves as a means to bridge gaps between the more educated and the less educated, the rich and the poor, the governors and the governed—to say nothing of the two separate library systems. Most important, it charts a course for addressing the present privation in Harare's public libraries.

Since there are a number of stakeholders involved, including government agencies and ministries, the municipality, the community, and nongovernmental organizations, each of these has a clear role in the sense of ensuring that the model works. For instance, the central government still has its broad role to champion policies that ensure that issues of equity and access to libraries are addressed. Some of its departments, like the Department of Physical Planning in the Ministry of Local Government, Rural and Urban Development, have the role to advise the city of Harare and sister local authorities in the Greater Harare region about the proper siting of libraries.

However, the community-led model would enable more consistency in management, training, human resources management, and salaries administration. The municipality will still play the role of an enabler; what is needed in this development is a sound system ensuring transparent and accountable management. This breaks the current closed-door system characterizing municipal management in Harare.

The proposed model is not a matter of privatizing the libraries. Far from it: rather, it is that of "communitarizing" them. Perhaps the monopoly of municipal control will have been converted to a monopoly on enabling. Under normal conditions, it would apply more to Low-Income Area libraries; however, in this time of rebuilding it applies to both these and those in the High-Income Areas.

The model outlines a participative approach, one that has been used broadly elsewhere in general development efforts—notably in South Africa—with some success.[13] In fact, such a model has already worked in some church organizations in Harare where subsidiary community branch churches run their own affairs (autonomous assemblies) but they all get their instructions/guides for conduct from a central office, the headquarters.

Although some communities will do well in a more robust way than others in such a venture, yet on the basis of equity such performance and outcome is a natural one. Through empowered engagement and active participation with their public libraries, communities could come to better know their own capacities and limits, and to respect who they are. What is important is that they realize these lessons and adjust accordingly.

NOTES

1. Gibbs Y. Kanyongo., "Zimbabwe's Public Education System Reforms: Successes and Challenges," *International Education Journal*, 6, no. 1 (2005): 65–74.

2. John Welford, "The Development of Community Libraries in Zimbabwe," *Helium*, March 23, 2009, www.httpwww.helium.com/items/1387300-development-of-rural -community-libraries-in-zimbabwe.

3. Cecil Mapfumo, "Private schools boom in Zimbabwe," *African Business* no. 369, (November 2010), 50–51.

4. Kanyongo, "Zimbabwe's Public Education System Reforms," 73.

5. J. Chisenga, *The Use of ICTs in African Public Libraries: A Survey of Ten Countries in Anglophone Africa* (Oxford: International Network for the Availability of Scientific Publications, 2004).

6. C. T. Chisita, *Public Libraries as Engines for Socio-Economic Development and Sustainable Social Cohesion: Case Study of Harare* (Harare: Harare Polytechnic, 2010), 43.

7. "The Economy of Zimbabwe," *Wikipedia*, http://en.wikipedia.org/wiki/Economy _of_Zimbabwe.

8. "The Browne Issue System," *Wikipedia,* http://en.wikipedia.org/wiki/Browne _Issue_System.

9. Aissa Issak, *Public Libraries in Africa: A Report and Annotated Bibliography* (Oxford: International Network for the Availability of Scientific Publications, 2000); Chisenga, *The Use of ICTs.*

10. Chisenga, *The Use of ICTs.*

11. In Issak, *Public Libraries in Africa.*

12. A. Nhema, *Demand for Libraries Increases in Zimbabwe City of Harare Libraries* (London: Book Aid International, 2010).

13. I. Davids, F. Theron, and K. J. Maphunyen, *Participatory Development in South Africa: A Development Management Perspective* (Pretoria: Van Schaik, 2005); Betsie Greyling, "Model for Community Participation in African Libraries to Preserve Indigenous Knowledge," paper for KM Africa Conference, Nairobi, 2007.

chapter fourteen

Pilar Martinez

Engaging communities, making a difference
Edmonton Public Library's community-led service philosophy

n 2005, the Edmonton Public Library (EPL) articulated a strategy to become "a socially responsible institution, a participant and an active initiator in community dialogue and development."[1] This strategy was enabled by means of an action plan that included finding ways to better serve those with "no place to go," continuing to develop staff understandings of communities and neighborhoods, and developing a community development strategy that included an expectation that staff spend time interacting and working with community groups.[2]

Through a network of 17 service points, the EPL serves an urban population of over 782,000, and just over 1 million in the metropolitan region. As the second-largest city in Alberta after Calgary, Edmonton is the provincial capital and widely known as "Festival City" because of its thriving arts and culture scene and numerous, year-round festivals. The library employs 435.8 full-time equivalent staff and holds approximately 3,500,000 physical and online library items. In 2011 the EPL logged over 14 million visits with 13.4 million items borrowed, making it Edmonton's largest lender of all forms of information and entertainment. Also in 2011, EPL provided over 10,500 programs for all ages and interests and collaborated with numerous community partners to provide joint programs.

The EPL is the first urban library in Canada to implement a systemwide community-led service philosophy, with nineteen community librarians working at service points throughout the library. The library's "community-led service philosophy" was initially defined as a way to build relationships and to improve the EPL's ability to identify customer strengths and meet customer needs, with a focus on anyone facing barriers to using library services. "Anyone facing barriers" could include homeless and socially excluded people, or those who simply lacked awareness of library service, but also—for example—a middle-class mom who had had a bad customer experience during a program and did not want to return to the library. This broad approach has allowed service points to prioritize, within the EPL's overall strategic directions, services based on the needs of their specific communities.

A community-led approach to service provision was not entirely new at the EPL. Over the past several years, EPL staff had worked collaboratively with communities in many ways, building relationships and developing services based on individual and community needs. In particular, the EPL had established formal partnerships with the separate and public school districts and the Centre for Family Literacy, and EPL staff had a long history of working with schools and various interagency groups. However, these efforts had not been consistently and strategically applied across the EPL system.

Efforts at implementing a more integrated, systemwide, and strategic approach to community-led work at the EPL were inspired in part by both John Pateman's work in the United Kingdom and by Canada's Working Together Project. Pateman, the founder of the journal *Information for Social Change,* has long worked in the areas of social exclusion and libraries as forces for social change.[3] The 2004–2008 Working Together Project had involved the Vancouver, Regina, Toronto, and Halifax public libraries in forging a community development approach to library services and reducing barriers for socially vulnerable communities.[4] The EPL relied on the *Working Together Community-Led Libraries Toolkit* as a valuable point of reference in formulating its strategy.[5]

However, distinctions from the Working Together approach emerged at the EPL in three main ways: the EPL's model is a systemwide framework used by all staff in varying degrees ("one library, one staff"), promoting community service as a shared value; EPL's community librarians are expected to do community work both inside and outside library walls; and EPL's focus extends beyond socially excluded populations to include anyone who faces barriers to library service.

The expectation was established that all public services managers become more engaged with their communities. Also, the EPL hired its first community development librarian intern, tasked with working with Edmonton's inner-city agencies in order to research best practices on community development and social responsibility; identify barriers and potential solutions for more inclusive and accessible approaches; identify staff training needs that meet the vision of a socially inclusive library; and develop recommendations for an ongoing community development strategy at the EPL.

In addition to these initiatives, between December 2008 and December 2009, the EPL created thirteen new community librarian positions by redirecting existing positions and later redesigned four existing adult services librarian positions to also reflect a community-led service expectation. These seventeen community librarians were commissioned without definitive job descriptions in place at the time—a deliberate exercise as the EPL wanted to build a community-led approach from the grassroots after gaining some experience working in and with the community. After six months of experience, a basic framework was established, and focused discussions about staff roles, community profiles, communication, and evaluation began to take place.

The EPL Community-Led Service Philosophy Toolkit

In August 2009, the EPL established a team to produce a *Community-Led Service Philosophy* (CLSP) *Toolkit* that would summarize the historical and philosophical context for the EPL's approach and offer a practical framework through which all EPL staff could understand and implement the new service philosophy. The team borrowed a phrase from Vancouver Public Library's Annette DeFaveri to identify community-led work as "connecting, consulting and working collaboratively with community members to understand the needs of the community and to inform the direction of library work and policies."[6] The EPL's goal became to strengthen its communities by connecting, consulting, and collaborating with these communities so that library services could better meet community and individual needs.

On the continuum of community involvement, the EPL's *CLSP Toolkit* situates the library's participation at the level where individuals and organizations influence library priorities. By building relationships with people and organizations, library staff members develop a better understanding of community needs and can better design services that meet those needs. Part of this process involves developing a thorough understanding of the library's communities and listening to what individuals and groups tell the EPL. It also involves working collaboratively with agencies and organizations to provide space for nonlibrary programs that meet community needs. The model used by the EPL is based on one used by the Tamarack Institute for Community Engagement. It emphasizes the distinctions between passive, reactive, participative, empowered, and leadership-oriented engagement, and the nature and degree of community involvement in each. Where community members can be informed in the *passive* model, provide input in the *reactive*, influence in the *participative*, and share in the tasks at hand in the *empowered*, the *leadership* model allows residents to initiate and lead on projects, with support from the library.[7]

A key principle in developing the EPL's *Community-Led Service Philosophy Toolkit* was staff involvement. Once an initial draft of the toolkit was completed, the EPL held two celebrations, inviting staff to provide feedback and brainstorm ideas around each section of the toolkit. Much of this feedback was incorporated into the current draft, which will continue to evolve and change according to ongoing analysis and evaluation. The "Community Profiles" section of the toolkit has already been modified to reflect the results of a debate over the level of detail and complexity required. Although most staff would like as much detail as possible, the EPL has limited the number of data elements in order to ensure a feasible and practical process. Ongoing use and review of the profiles will help the library grasp what additional data, if any, is required.

The toolkit addresses the various levels of EPL staff contribution by job function and outlines the different expectations for staff throughout the system. While all staff members are expected to understand and adopt the community-led service philosophy, it affects each operational activity differently.

Practical application

The application of the community-led service philosophy varies according to the nature of the communities served by the various library branches. Community librarians work with organizations representing a range of individuals and groups including Aboriginal, multicultural, Somali, seniors, newcomers, youth, students, preschoolers, persons with mental health issues, women who have been abused, and the city of Edmonton. In 2011 community librarians worked with over 310 organizations in Edmonton, spending an average of 20 hours a week on relationship building (not including programming with these organizations). These collaborations have yielded some significant impacts.

For over a year, two YMCA youth workers have worked twice weekly from the downtown Stanley A. Milner Library, connecting with 30 to 40 at-risk youth per week. Through contact with these youth workers, one girl was able to enter the YMCA Transitions program and is about to complete grade 12. Two others have entered a YMCA preemployment training program. Seeing the posters and having the opportunity to develop relationships with the workers in the library allowed these youth to take the necessary steps to enter these programs. The EPL's collaboration with the YMCA has provided a valuable resource for these young library users.

The EPL Book Borrowing Project at the Edmonton Institution for Women (EIFW) and its work with the Remand Centre are significant examples of how the EPL's commitment to community-led work is reaching populations that have been traditionally excluded from library services. In collaboration with the Greater Edmonton Library Association's (GELA's) Prison Library Committee, the EPL loans books to incarcerated women that may be returned to the prison library. There are significant security issues in accessing this community, but the EPL's community librarian's relationship with the librarian and the collaboration with GELA have made this project successful. Through monthly visits, the librarian meets with the women, learns how the library can better meet their needs, and works with the prison librarian to harmonize borrowing procedures and solicit feedback. Over a short period, the number of EIFW Library users has grown, and there is always a line of women waiting at the doors for the librarian's scheduled visit. These visits also provide the opportunity to support reintegrating populations back into the community through promoting EPL services, particularly computer and technology support services.

Other collaborations have resulted in significant systemwide practice and policy changes geared toward reducing barriers to library services: the EPL created a six-month computer/Internet pass card for individuals who are ineligible to obtain a full library membership because they do not have a fixed address; an agency referral letter was created allowing agency clients with no permanent address to obtain a library card using the agency's address; a 5-item-limit library card was created for customers who have difficulty returning items; and the EPL revised its customer conduct policy to diminish the rigidity of its provisions. All of these initiatives reflect a commitment to reduce barriers, to be socially responsible, and to establish policies based on self-identified community needs.

What the EPL has learned/challenges

As word spread of the EPL's community-led service philosophy, enthusiastic requests from all over the city for all types of commitments came pouring in. Likewise, there was a sense internally that community librarians could take responsibility for numerous projects and activities. For example, the EPL was asked to sit on committees looking at establishing memorials for homeless who have passed away and to be involved in identification storage for homeless individuals. Careful evaluation was required to make certain that requests fit with the library's mission and to ensure effective use of community librarians' time. Declining external requests has been a struggle for the EPL as, like other public libraries, there is a tendency to err on the side of saying yes to them. Community librarians have also been challenged to reach out beyond the familiar to encourage new relationships among different types of groups and organizations. Connecting with new organizations takes time, patience, and persistence. At the same time, it can be difficult to build relationships with some organizations due to the interest level or operational constraints of their staff. This has been a particular challenge when the community is identified by the EPL as a priority.

Another challenge for community librarians has been learning to work within the ambiguity of a model that is under development and without clear parameters regarding how to do community-led work. In some cases, new community librarians lacked an awareness of their own internal service point community and were initiating services and programs that were already in place. This created an opportunity to frame the community-led framework more broadly and ensure the crucial step of familiarization with the EPL internal community first. This meant taking time to communicate with colleagues, try new things, and take risks. In retrospect, this is why the EPL has been so successful: community librarians truly had the freedom to "try anything"—and they certainly did!

Redesigning librarian positions from a traditional to a community-led role has not been altogether straightforward. It has required critical thinking about the job requirements in specific work areas, since not all positions can meet the expectation of allocating 70 percent of their time to community-led activities. At the same time, some EPL librarians in traditional roles have felt undervalued. The fact that traditional librarian roles at the EPL have been evolving—a reduced focus on collections with centralized collection development, decreased specialization, and more generalist roles—has compounded this challenge. Conversations with staff continue in order to explore various ways contributions can be made and to find the appropriate balance of roles.

The concept of community-led librarianship is inherently ambiguous. It was initially challenging for many EPL staff not only to understand the community librarians' roles, but to understand how they could implement the community-led service philosophy into their own roles. To facilitate this understanding, it was important to foster a sense of community and encourage open conversation within service points. Finding creative ways to involve nonlibrarian staff in community work, such as accompanying community librarians to meetings and delivering programs for community groups, has helped to ensure that EPL staff are all on board with the community-led service philosophy.

Making a difference

There have been measurable outcomes, such as a marked increase in the circulation of particular collections and in program attendance, which can be reasonably attributed to the increased visibility of the EPL within specific communities; nevertheless, it can be challenging to identify the impact of these outcomes. An important part of a community librarian's work is evaluating the success of community collaborations by assessing feedback from community partners. As the EPL moves forward, the focus will be on measuring the impact of this collaborative work.

It is apparent that the EPL has gained widespread community support and developed strong library advocates as a result of the community librarians' relationship building. This was demonstrated when the library was facing potential cutbacks during the 2010 municipal budget public hearings. Speakers from the Native Healing Friendship Centre and the Boyle Street Cooperative spoke passionately about the library's impact, arguing that the EPL was the only place where homeless people were welcomed and that the EPL had helped prevent Aboriginal youth from being on the street, potentially engaging in drugs and prostitution. These impacts are difficult to measure without complex studies, but, using the Basic Logic Model of evaluation, this will be a major focus for the EPL in 2012 and beyond.[8]

Future plans and next steps

The next phase for the community-led service philosophy at the EPL is a focus on evaluation, both at the community librarian and service point levels, as well as the overall systemwide level. The expertise of the newly hired manager of assessment and research will greatly assist with this process. In addition, community librarians will undertake a regular process of evaluating their relationships and impact with each organization—something that to date has been undertaken in an ad hoc fashion. These evaluations, along with the Basic Logic Model, will help both the EPL and its communities to determine whether the library is meeting identified needs, and to develop an improved understanding of outcomes.

In 2011 the EPL completed all service-point community profiles, consisting of demographic factors and trends, service area descriptions, and community assets. The next phase will involve the application of these profiles to the EPL's community-led work, library service development, and obtaining feedback on profile relevance.

Evaluating the migration of traditional librarian roles to community librarian roles also will be undertaken, and conversations around integrating a community-led focus into all jobs will be a continued focus. Finally, sharing successes, failures, and opportunities will continue through the use of staff blogs and meetings with managers, librarians, and other staff.

Summary

The development of the community-led service philosophy at the Edmonton Public Library has been a two-and-a-half-year inclusive process which has had the benefit of a strong foundation of relationship-building and collaboration laid over many decades. The community-led service philosophy has been a grassroots initiative involving consultation with staff from all aspects of the organization, the involvement of many public services staff, and, most notably, the practice, knowledge, and experience of the EPL's community development librarian intern and the first EPL community librarians. For the most part, Edmonton's communities have embraced the library's involvement and clearly see the benefits of the community-led service philosophy. The Edmonton Public Library's community-led service philosophy is an evolving process reflecting the learning and growth of the library and the dynamic nature of the individuals and communities it serves.

NOTES

1. Edmonton Public Library, *Enriching People's Lives: Edmonton Public Library Strategic Directions 2006–2010*. www.epl.ca/ResourcesPDF/StrategicPlan2006-10.pdf.

2. Edmonton Public Library, *Edmonton Public Library Business Plan*, 2006–2010.

3. "John Pateman—Cuban Libraries Solidarity Group," *Information for Social Change*, www.libr.org/isc/profile.html.

4. Libraries in Communities, *Working Together* (Vancouver: Libraries in Communities, 2009), www.librariesincommunities.ca/?page_id=8.

5. Libraries in Communities, *Libraries in Communities Toolkit* (Vancouver: Libraries in Communities, 2008), www.librariesincommunities.ca/resources/Community-Led_Libraries_Toolkit.pdf.

6. Annette DeFaveri, "Community Development in a Library Context" (audio conference), Working Together, www.librariesincommunities.ca/?page_id=4.

7. Paul Born, "Community Engagement and Systems of Change," presentation at "Leading Together in Chaotic Times," Communities Collaborating Institute, 2010.

8. For example, see the "Logic Model" page at the University of Wisconsin Extension, www.uwex.edu/ces/pdande/evaluation/evallogicmodel.html.

contributors

MAIJA BERNDTSON has served as the director of the Helsinki City Library, Central Library for Public Libraries in Finland, since 1987. Berndtson was a jury member of the architecture competitions for the New Cultural Centre of Turin in 2000–2001, the Stockholm Public Library in 2006–2007, and Deichman Library of the Oslo Public Library in 2009. She has been internationally active in different projects within European Union, such as PubliCA, Public Libraries Concerted Action in 1997–99. In 2008 she was granted the 2008 Nuutti Award in recognition of her lifetime of activities for the benefit of library users and in the development of library services. She was a member of the International Network of Public Libraries run by the Bertelsmann Foundation in 1998–2001, and during that time she wrote the *Management Self-Assessment* report in 1999 and *Dreaming the Future—Some Funky Ideas on Managing Tomorrow's Library* in 2001. She coauthored *Virtual Impact on the Physical Library: Visions for Intelligent Change* in 2002. She has written many articles in Finnish library journals and has lectured in many international conferences all over Europe.

INNOCENT CHIRISA is a lecturer at the Department of Rural and Urban Planning, University of Zimbabwe, and teaches courses in regional economics. He holds a master of science degree in rural and urban planning and is studying toward a doctorate in social studies at the University of Zimbabwe. Chirisa has published several papers in the areas of housing, urban informality, demographic change in Africa, and peri-urban stewardship.

DENISE CLARK has nearly twenty years' experience working in the nonprofit sector. She has secured more than $100 million in grant funding for humanitarian relief, education, construction, health, youth development, literacy, and micro-finance programs. Clark has also provided trainings across the United States, Europe, and Africa in nonprofit management, strategic fund-raising, and evaluation. In her seven years of working with the Queens Public Library, she has secured more than $25 million in city, state, and federal grants.

MICHAEL DUDLEY is the indigenous and urban services librarian at the University of Winnipeg. Following nearly a decade working in public libraries in both Edmonton and Calgary, Alberta, Dudley obtained a graduate degree in city planning. For 11 years, Michael worked at the Institute of Urban Studies where he engaged in community-based, public interest research, and operated the Institute's library. He is the editorial board chair for *Plan Canada* magazine (the official publication of the Canadian Institute of Planners); a regular book reviewer for the *Winnipeg Free Press;* and a regular contributor to the urban planning website *Planetizen*.

JULIE BIANDO EDWARDS is an assistant professor and ethnic studies librarian and multicultural coordinator at the Mansfield Library, University of Montana in Missoula. She has a master of arts in English from the University of Connecticut and received her master of science in library and information science from the University of Illinois, Urbana-Champaign, in 2005. She began her career as a public librarian and has research interests in human rights and librarianship as well as in libraries and community. She is the coauthor, with Stephan P. Edwards, of "Libraries, Community Life, and Cultural Identity," delivered at the "Libraries from a Human Rights Perspective" conference in Ramallah, Palestine, 2008, and "Culture and the New Iraq: The Iraq National Library and Archives, Imagined Community, and the Future of the Iraqi Nation," published in *Libraries & the Cultural Record,* August 2008. She recently coedited a book, *Beyond Article 19: Libraries and Social and Cultural Rights,* published in 2010.

VANESSA N. FRANCIS serves as the assistant director of government and community affairs (GCA) for Johns Hopkins University. Before joining GCA she spent eight years working in strategic urban/regional planning and research in the Maryland and Washington, DC, areas. Most recently, Francis served as the senior planner for the Maryland National Capitol Park and Planning Commission in the Montgomery County Planning Department. There she was responsible for project management, monitored legislative matters, and assisted with projects focusing on healthy communities and land use planning. A Baltimore City native, Francis received her bachelor's degree in political science and her master's degree in city and regional planning at Morgan State University. She is a current member of the Enoch Pratt Library's Advisory Council.

MATTHEW EVAN HAVENS is a research associate with the Institute of Urban Studies at the University of Winnipeg. His work has included sustainability planning for the northern Canadian town of Churchill, First Nations economic development, and research for a national study on homelessness in Canada. He has a BA in geography from the University of Winnipeg and is currently studying the geography and politics of energy systems. He has examined initiatives that communities across the globe are taking to prepare for climate change and energy scarcity, and is currently involved with the startup of one of these initiatives, Transition Winnipeg. Matthew has given presentations on the topic of peak oil and also contributes book reviews to the *Winnipeg Free Press* on issues of energy, globalization, and the environment.

DR. GLEN HOLT is a writer and researcher for Holt Consulting. He wrote a quarterly column on library economics in *The Bottom Line* for eleven years and for the electronic journal *LLN* (*Library Leadership Network*) *Bulletin* for three years. He edited *Public Library Quarterly* for seven years, and is coauthor of a book on library cost-benefit analysis, another on library success stories, and a third on public library services for the poor. He was the CEO of the St. Louis Public Library for seventeen years. Holt is the winner of Public Library Association's Charlie Robinson Award (2003), given to a public library director for innovation and risk taking in management. Holt was a teacher and administrator at Washington University for thirteen years and at the University of Minnesota for five years. His BA is from Baker University, his MA and PhD from the University of Chicago. His consultancies have included museums, historical societies, school systems, libraries, foundations, legal firms, and city governments.

JENNIFER HOYER has given elementary school story times in low-income immigrant neighborhoods (Westmount Elementary School, Westmount, Quebec) and worked at a privately funded community library in downtown Montréal (Atwater Library and Computer Centre) and the special library of a nonprofit social policy think tank in Alberta (Edmonton Social Planning Council). She is passionate about equitable information access and teaching information skills in nonacademic environments. Her previous career was as a performing musician, and she is involved in a number of projects related to the historical performance of Renaissance and Baroque music. She has taught musicology as a sessional instructor at King's University College in Edmonton, Alberta.

MARY WILKINS JORDAN is an assistant professor at Simmons College in Boston Massachusetts. Her teaching and research areas revolve around effective administration of libraries. Prior to entering academia, she worked as a public library director and administrator and was an attorney.

MELLER LANGFORD is the deputy director for public services at the Houston Public Library. She holds a master's degree of library science from Ball State University in Muncie, Indiana, and has over thirty years of experience in libraries, including sixteen years as a library administrator. She joined the Houston Public Library in 1987 as a branch manager and has served in several managerial capacities during her tenure there. Langford has broad experience and knowledge of library operations, including management of neighborhood libraries, special collections, and outreach. She is currently serving on the Texas Library Association's Executive Board.

DR. RHEA BROWN LAWSON is the executive director of the Houston Public Library. The Houston Public Library serves over 2.2 million people, is the largest library in the state of Texas, and ranks seventh among the nation's largest public library systems in terms of population served. Before moving to Houston, Lawson served in a number of capacities, including deputy director of the Detroit Public Library; chief of the Brooklyn Public Library's Central Library in Brooklyn, New York; administrator of lifelong services at the Enoch Pratt Free Library in Baltimore, Maryland; and assistant professor in the School of Library and Information Studies at Wayne State University in Detroit, Michigan. Since taking the helm of the Houston Public Library, Lawson has overseen several new state-of-the-art construction and renovation capital projects, including the launch of four HPL-Express locations, an innovative new library service model that is the first of its kind in the nation; and the launch of the library's third special collection, the African American Library at the Gregory School, which will serve as a repository for the history and culture of African Americans in Houston.

PILAR MARTINEZ has over twenty years' experience in public and regional libraries. As the executive director of public services at the Edmonton Public Library, she leads the planning and implementation of strategies for services, staffing, and collections there. With the support of the EPL's community librarians and managers, Pilar is responsible for leading the implementation and evaluation of the community-led service philosophy framework. The EPL is now delivering services that more closely align with community needs, both within and beyond library walls, as a result of this initiative. Martinez is passionate about social responsibility and community-led library service.

DEBORAH OLLEY MURPHY has worked at Queens Library for nearly four years. In her current capacity as assistant director of marketing communications, Olley Murphy edits Queens Library's award-winning flagship publication, *Enrich Your Life*. She also oversees all marketing collateral and campaigns for Queens Library, writes pieces for trade publications, and maintains the library's brand through print advertising and other efforts. A trained librarian, Olley Murphy has also worked in fund-raising (prospect research and grant writing) and health care communications, and founded an oral history business, Visiting with Words.

MELISSA RAUSEO is the teen librarian at the Peabody Institute Library in Peabody, Massachusetts. She has been a patron, a fan, and an employee of public libraries her whole life. Her library interests revolve around libraries as partners in community development and youth development. She has done consulting projects for public school districts and library organizations on topics relating to young adult literature, library programming, and teen advisory boards.

ROOSEVELT WEEKS is deputy director of administration at the Houston Public Library. Weeks, a six-year HPL veteran, is also a member of the Houston Public Library Executive Leadership Team. He was promoted to the deputy director position in 2006. Prior to this assignment, Weeks served as chief technology officer for the Houston Public Library. He currently serves on the Southeast Houston Community Development Corporation board and works closely with the Houston READ Commission and the Houston Independent School District. He also serves on the city of Houston's Health Benefit Advisory Committee, SAP Steering Committee, and the IT Management Committee.

MONIQUE WORONIAK has been an outreach services librarian with the Winnipeg Public Library since 2007, where she has developed and delivered community-based services for Aboriginal peoples and newcomers to Canada. She holds a BA in political studies from the University of Manitoba and an MLIS degree from the School of Information Management at Dalhousie University, where her thesis focused on information management and First Nations communities in Canada.

index

You may also be interested in

A STRONG FUTURE FOR PUBLIC LIBRARY USE AND EMPLOYMENT

José-Marie Griffiths and Donald W. King

"This book is an excellent resource for library administrators. . . . Plan to take it to your next board or budget hearing."—*Public Libraries*

ISBN: 978-0-8389-3588-0
160 pages / 8.5" x 11"

GRASSROOTS LIBRARY ADVOCACY

Lauren Comito, Aliqae Geraci, and Christian Zabriskie

ISBN: 978-0-8389-1134-1

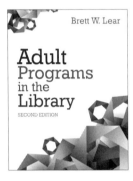

ADULT PROGRAMS IN THE LIBRARY, SECOND EDITION

Brett W. Lear

ISBN: 978-0-8389-1140-2

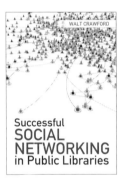

SUCCESSFUL SOCIAL NETWORKING IN PUBLIC LIBRARIES

Walt Crawford

ISBN: 978-0-8389-1167-9

REFLECTING ON THE FUTURE OF ACADEMIC AND PUBLIC LIBRARIES

Edited by Peter Hernon and Joseph R. Matthews

ISBN: 978-0-8389-1187-7

GETTING STARTED WITH EVALUATION

Peter Hernon, Robert E. Dugan, and Joseph R. Matthews

ISBN: 978-0-8389-1195-2

HOW LIBRARIES MAKE TOUGH CHOICES IN DIFFICULT TIMES: PURPOSEFUL ABANDONMENT

David Stern

ISBN: 978-1-84334-701-9

Order today at **alastore.ala.org** or **866-746-7252!**

ALA Store purchases fund advocacy, awareness, and accreditation programs for library professionals worldwide.